"'A journey of a thousand miles begins with a single
DaoDeJing. In this illuminating book on XinYi WuD
Arts'), (Master Wu guides us, step-by-step, on a jour
ultimate martial art—the art beyond fighting.) Through the
of the Three Treasures of Life—our bodies of flesh, energy, and spirit—
learn how to martial these precious resources in a way that benefits self and
other as one.)

Thanks to the kindness of his mentor, Grandmaster Zhao ShouRong,
Master Wu shares with us, for the first time in English print, ancient secrets of
the way of the martial heart)—handed down in China in an unbroken lineage
from master to disciple. Whether your interest lies primarily in the practice
or the philosophy, you will discover within these pages precious gems of
wisdom and power that will enrich your life."

—*Daniel Reid, best-selling author of* The Tao of Health, Sex, and Longevity
and The Tao of Detox, *and a leading expert of Eastern philosophy and medicine*

"As an aikido practitioner, I found lineage holder Master Zhongxian
Wu's latest book, *XinYi WuDao*, very fascinating. Providing an in-depth
explanation of the links between Daoism and Chinese martial arts, Master
Wu shows his deep dedication and unique knowledge of these two ancient
traditions. There are many similar links that can be made between aikido and
its philosophy, which makes this book a fantastic source of inspiration for all
aikido practitioners."

—*Jan Nevelius Shihan (sixth Dan Aikikai Tokyo),*
Chinese medicine practitioner and author

"Dai Family XinYi is a rare martial art in China. In this book, Master Wu
reveals many techniques that have never been made available to the public.
He explains the Dao theories in a very easy to understand way, as well as the
basic form and the movements of WuXing Quan Mu and BaGua XinJing.
He also describes the principles, breath, and visualization in detail for each
movement. This is a very valuable book for readers to trace back the origin
and hidden treasure of the powerful Xingyi Quan."

—*Master C.S. Tang, senior Xingyi Quan, Bagua Quan, and Yi Quan*
expert and researcher, and author of The Mysterious Power of
Xingyi Quan *and* The Complete Book of Yiquan

XinYi WuDao

by the same author

Heavenly Stems and Earthly Branches—TianGan DiZhi
The Heart of Chinese Wisdom Traditions
Master Zhongxian Wu and Dr. Karin Taylor Wu
Foreword by Fei BingXun
ISBN 978 1 84819 151 8
eISBN 978 0 85701 158 9

Heavenly Stems and Earthly Branches—TianGan DiZhi
The Keys to the Sublime
Master Zhongxian Wu and Dr. Karin Taylor Wu
ISBN 978 1 84819 150 1 (card set)

Fire Dragon Meridian Qigong
Essential NeiGong for Health and Spiritual Transformation
Master Zhongxian Wu and Dr. Karin Taylor Wu
ISBN 978 1 84819 103 7
eISBN 978 0 85701 085 8

Chinese Shamanic Cosmic Orbit Qigong
Esoteric Talismans, Mantras, and Mudras in Healing and Inner Cultivation
Master Zhongxian Wu
ISBN 978 1 84819 056 6
eISBN 978 0 85701 059 9

The 12 Chinese Animals
Create Harmony in your Daily Life through Ancient Chinese Wisdom
Master Zhongxian Wu
ISBN 978 1 84819 031 3
eISBN 978 0 85701 015 5

Seeking the Spirit of The Book of Change
8 Days to Mastering a Shamanic Yijing (I Ching) Prediction System
Master Zhongxian Wu
Foreword by Daniel Reid
ISBN 978 1 84819 020 7
eISBN 978 0 85701 007 0

Vital Breath of the Dao
Chinese Shamanic Tiger Qigong—Laohu Gong
Master Zhongxian Wu
Foreword by Chungliang Al Huang
ISBN 978 1 84819 000 9
eISBN 978 0 85701 110 7

XinYi WuDao

HEART–MIND

THE DAO OF MARTIAL ARTS

Master Zhongxian Wu

Foreword by Grandmaster Zhao ShouRong

SINGING
DRAGON

LONDON AND PHILADELPHIA

First published in 2014
by Singing Dragon
an imprint of Jessica Kingsley Publishers
73 Collier Street
London N1 9BE, UK
and
400 Market Street, Suite 400
Philadelphia, PA 19106, USA

www.singingdragon.com

Library of Congress Cataloging in Publication Data
Wu, Zhongxian.
  Xinyi wudao : heart-mind - the Dao of martial arts / Master
Zhongxian Wu ; foreword by Grandmaster
Zhao ShouRong.
    pages cm
  ISBN 978-1-84819-206-5 (alk. paper)
  1. Martial arts--Philosophy. 2. Tao. I. Title.
  GV1101.W8 2014
  796.8--dc23
                        2013041887

British Library Cataloguing in Publication Data
A CIP catalogue record for this book is available from the British Library

ISBN 978 1 84819 206 5
eISBN 978 0 85701 156 5

Printed and bound in Great Britain by Bell & Bain Ltd, Glasgow

謹以此書
獻給我的
師父趙守榮
師母喬金秀

This book is dedicated to
ShiFu Zhao ShouRong
and ShiMu Qiao JinXiu

Author's Notes

- True to Daoist philosophy, the Dai Family XinYi martial arts system emphasizes the cultivation of Yin power, generated deep within. As such, in this book I have chosen to use "she" when referring to those who have truly mastered the art and "he" for those who focus on combat and muscular power.

- I have chosen to capitalize all Chinese *PinYin* words and phrases throughout this book. On first introduction, each will appear translated alongside the appropriate Chinese characters.

- All Chinese *PinYin* words and phrases will be italicized with the exception of proper names and widely used Chinese words, for example Dao, Yin, Yang, Qigong, Taiji, XinYi, etc.

- When the following words are capitalized—Five Elements, Element, Water, Wood, Fire, Earth, and Metal—they refer specifically to the Chinese *WuXing* 五行 (Five Elements).

- Passages of Chinese logograms are presented in the traditional style—from top to bottom, right to left. The modern *PinYin* reads in the conventional style—left to right.

Contents

Acknowledgments

A special thanks to *ZhongGuoQingNianBao* 中國青年報 (China Youth) journalist Zhen PingPing 鄭萍萍 and to Cain Carroll for permission to put some of their photos from our 2011 XinYi China trip into the introduction of this book.

Once again, I'd like to convey my appreciation to Jessica Kingsley and her Singing Dragon for helping to bring another one of my books into reality.

As always, my gratitude is bestowed upon my teachers, masters, and family for supporting me on my path. I offer this book with a humble bow to my master Zhao ShouRong 趙守榮 and his family for their generosity and openheartedness, especially with respect to my study, training, and teaching of the Dai Family XinYi system. I'd also like to especially thank Master Zhao's son, Zhao KouZhi 趙扣志, for his friendship and help over the years.

I am very grateful for this new chapter in my life and for the long stretches of quiet content I experienced while writing this book. Each day I feel as though my wife and I are living within an extraordinary painting—the Stockholm archipelago is beautiful, peaceful, and powerful and has served as a great source of inspiration for my writing.

And to my wife, Karin Taylor Wu, I'd like to express my deepest love for your presence in our life together. I am sure that without your thoughtful commentary, perceptive questioning, editing expertise, and artistic photography, this book would not be here!

滅，戴奎先生終將其拳傳出戴家，吾師祁縣魯村高升禎先生為其開門弟子。吾幸於14歲時拜於本村高師門下，65年專修戴家拳，對此拳仍愛不釋手。

戴家拳以道武雙修為特色，如入門混元樁即以固養靈根培育丹田炁入手，為整個拳繫打下堅實基礎。此拳既可用於搏擊又可頤養天年，修真合道。心意拳經曰：

養靈根而動心者敢將也

固靈根而靜心者修道也

吳忠賢繫吾嫡傳弟子，在道武修煉上頗具天賦，能學以至用，舉一反三。吾勵之著述多載，今以《心意武道》一書示世，乃一大惠舉，願更多人能因此而得益於戴氏心意六合拳之功用。

趙守榮

癸巳秋

於山西太谷

道武雙全

武藝雖精竅不真

費盡心機枉勞神

祖师留下真妙術

只待苦志有恆人

心意六合拳經

心意拳自道家華山隱仙派陳搏祖師傳出，經宋周侗先生傳至武穆王岳飛得大顯其威，後匿跡數百年。

明末清初，有山西蒲州姬隆峰先生訪師終南得武穆拳經，歸而依讻悉心修煉多年，使斯技重光。後傳曹繼武先生，曹先生再傳祁縣戴隆邦先生。戴先生结合家傳之武學及道家丹功，將心意拳發揮成自成特色之演煉方式，即後世所尊之戴氏心意六合拳。

由於此拳實戰性極強，戴隆邦先生告戒其後人不可輕易外傳以免落入非人之手，故其術限傳於戴家而外人難窺一斑。經其子戴二閭傳於佺戴梁棟，戴梁棟傳子戴奎。苦於膝下無子，為不使斯術堙

Foreword

The Union of Dao and Martial Arts

Zhao ShouRong 趙守榮

Lacking the internal secrets, great physical martial skills
⎛Will waste your energy and exhaust your spirit ⎠
The ancestral master left this marvelous art
Which lies in wait for the mindful person with a constant heart

XINYI SIX UNIONS MARTIAL ARTS CLASSIC

The XinYi martial arts system was brought forth from Daoist hermits into the general public by the ancestral master of the Daoist *HuaShanYinXianPai* 華山隱仙派 (Flower Mountain Hidden Immortal Lineage), Ancestral Master Chen Tuan 祖師陳搏. During the Song Dynasty (960–1279 CE), Master Zhou Tong 周侗 passed the system on to Yue Fei 岳飛. Yue Fei became one of the greatest military generals in Chinese history. He used his superior knowledge of the XinYi system to train the soldiers in his powerful army and lead the defeat of the northern invaders. For political reasons, the XinYi martial arts system then disappeared from the public eye for several hundreds of years. At the end of the Ming Dynasty (1368–1644 CE) and beginning of the Qing Dynasty (1644–1912 CE), Master Ji LongFeng 姬隆峰, from the *Pu* 蒲 region of ShanXi 山西 province, traveled to ZhongNan 終南 Mountain seeking a martial arts teacher. There, he discovered the XinYi Martial Arts Classic written by General Yue Fei. After returning home, Master Ji spent many years studying and practicing the skills from this martial arts classic and was able to bring the XinYi martial arts system back to life. Later, he passed the art to Master Chao JiWu 曹繼武, who then passed it on to Master Dai LongBang 戴隆邦 from Qi 祁 County in ShanXi province. Due to his great proficiency in his own family's tradition of martial arts and Daoist internal alchemy cultivation, Master Dai took mastery of the XinYi system to a new level. The depth and clarity of his understanding of the XinYi martial arts system was widely respected by other martial artists and became known specifically as Dai Family XinYi Six Unions Martial Arts.

As the Dai Family XinYi system teaches such formidable combat skills, Master Dai, concerned about allowing such a powerful fighting aptitude to fall into the wrong hands, staunchly warned his descendants against teaching the art to anyone outside of the Dai Family. His son Dai ErLü 戴二閭 passed the art to his nephew, Dai LiangDong 戴梁棟, and Dai LiangDong taught it to his son, Dai Kui 戴奎. As Dai Kui did not have any children, he eventually decided it was better to let the art out of the Dai Family than have it die out. My master, Gao ShengZhen 高升禎, from Lu 魯 village in Qi 祁 County, was his disciple—the first person outside of the Dai Family to be taught this art. I was born and raised in the same village as Master Gao and, luckily, I became his disciple when I was 14 years old. For the last 65 years, I have practiced only Dai Family XinYi and it still brings me great joy each day.

Grandmaster Dai Kui
Fourth generation lineage holder

Grandmaster Gao ShengZhen
Fifth generation lineage holder

The defining characteristic of Dai Family XinYi is the union of the Dao and martial arts. From the very start of their XinYi training, students learn physical postures that help them understand the deeper layers of meaning of the system as a whole, as well as how to apply the system in their martial arts practice, to defeat others, nourish their own lives, experience longevity, and for their Daoist internal cultivation practice. The XinYi Martial Arts Classic states:

Nourished by your spiritual root
Guided by your heart
The enemy is defeated

Unwavering spiritual root
And a tranquil heart
To cultivate the Dao

Master Zhongxian Wu 吳忠賢 is my disciple. He is gifted with a unique genius as both a highly skilled martial artist and Daoist practitioner. When I teach him one, he takes in ten. I have been encouraging him to write a book on Dai Family XinYi for many years now. A great virtue, he has finally brought *XinYi WuDao* 心意武道 to the world. Through this book, I hope many people will gain benefits from learning Dai Family XinYi.

Zhao ShouRong 趙守榮[1]

Autumn, Year of Snake (2013)
ShanXi, TaiGu

---

1 Grandmaster Zhao ShouRong 趙守榮 is the sixth generation lineage holder of the Dai Family XinYi system.

Introduction

The Art of Peace[1]

其實貴和　名雖曰武

MingSuiYueWu QiShiGuiHe

Although it is called martial arts, it is in fact harmony

DAI LONGBANG 戴隆邦,
FOUNDER MASTER OF DAISHIXINYIQUAN 戴氏心意拳
(DAI FAMILY STYLE XINYI MARTIAL ARTS)

---

1   This introduction cites many passages from my article "Martial Arts, Qigong, and Shen 神 (Spiritual) Cultivation," which was first published in *Empty Vessel: A Journal of Daoist Philosophy and Practice*, Fall 2004.

I. The Dao of Martial Arts

People often ask me if I practice KungFu. "What kind of KungFu?" they wonder, after I tell them that I do. When I answer that I practice Qigong and Taiji, the typical response is a vague look of confusion. Most people regard KungFu as a hard and tough fighting skill and it is difficult for them to imagine that the gentle and slow movements of my Qigong and Taiji forms have any links to martial arts.

馳騁天下之至堅　天下之至柔

TianXiaZhiZhiRou ChiPingTianXiaZhiZhiJian[2]

The softest under Heaven controls the hardest under Heaven

This statement, from Chapter 43 of LaoZi's *DaoDeJing* 道德經, is the core principle of all my KungFu training. Through years and years of soft-style inner cultivation practice, I was gradually able to come to the understanding that (the original purpose of KungFu is not training to fight; rather, it is training to have the ability to stop a fight)—to alter the course of a violent situation and move it toward a peaceful resolution.

The word KungFu is the Wade-Giles Romanization for the Chinese phrase 功夫, which in the modern *PinYin* 拼音 system is GongFu. In Chinese folk culture, we commonly use this phrase in many situations—to describe time, as when it takes a lot of time to do something of worth; a skill, as when it takes considerable skill to master an art form; and martial arts, because it takes time and dedication to improve your martial arts skills. The literary term for martial arts is *WuShu* 武術. To help understand the true goal of martial arts, let's briefly analyze the symbolic meaning of *WuShu*.

---

2   LaoZi, *DaoDeJing*.

Wu 武 is commonly translated as "martial." The character is constructed of two radicals: *Zhi* 止, which means stop, and *Ge* 戈, a type of ancient Chinese weapon which is used to represent the military and martial arts. *ZhiGeWeiWu* 止戈为武,[3] one of the earliest definitions of *Wu*, means "stop fighting." This illustrates the original peaceful meaning of *Wu* 武 (martial) as true power, not the kind of force associated with the use of weapons. *Shu* 術 means an art, technique, or method. In other words, *WuShu* literally means the art of not fighting. A skilled martial artist can gain control of the situation without bringing damage to himself or to his opponent, without fighting, blocking, or punching. The most highly skilled martial artist uses her wisdom and strategy to subdue the enemy without ever needing to enter into battle. The *XiCi* 系辞 (the Appended Statements), one of the ten Confucian commentaries of the *YiJing* 易經 (also known as *I Ching* or *Book of Change*), states this best: *ShenWuBuSha* 神武不殺[4]—the martial artist of high spirit does not act through killing or fighting. This same principle is illustrated in the *Art of War*: "To subdue the enemy without fighting is the supreme excellence."[5]

We will gain clearer insight into the ultimate aim of the martial artist if we take a quick look at martial arts history. The martial arts were created and perfected long ago and were modeled after fundamental patterns of life. Prehistoric Chinese lived in accordance with the rhythms of nature, hunting for their livelihood and being able to fight for survival. For this life, it was necessary for them to develop acute awareness of their surroundings and of the limits and potentials of their own bodies. These people also had to understand the strengths and strategies of their own enemies and learn the means by which to best control them. Ancient China was also beset by wars between the varied states and tribes. Living in such conditions compelled these people to create training techniques for self-defense as well as for battle.

---

3 *Zhi* 止 (stop), *Ge* 戈 (weapon/military), *Wei* 为 (is/as), *Wu* 武 (military) is from Zuo QiuMing's 左丘明 (556–451 BCE) historical text *ZuoZhuan* 左傳.

4 *Shen* 神 (spirit), *Wu* 武 (martial), *Bu* 不 (not), *Sha* 殺 (kill).

5 SunZi, the author of this text, lived in the Warring States period around the same time as KongZi (Confucius): 551–479 BCE. It is believed that SunZi was born sometime between 550 BCE and 540 BCE.

The *Wu* 巫, enlightened sages and great shaman-kings of this time period whose discoveries influenced the development of all aspects of traditional Chinese culture, created a system of movements and body mechanics designed to safeguard others from harm. They ascertained that the virtue (i.e. function) of Heaven is to give birth to the Ten-Thousand-Things and to protect and preserve all life. The spiritual goal of the martial artist is to follow this Heavenly Way of peaceful living. These movements were intended to be a method to save a life, bring about peace in times of war, and move practitioners closer to the Dao.

II. The De of Martial Arts

There are numerous martial arts schools throughout China, from large, widely known schools such as *Shaolin* 少林, *Wudang* 武當, *Emei* 峨嵋, and *Huashan* 華山, to smaller schools that teach a localized regional form or particular family's style. Although different schools and different masters have their own teaching methods and techniques, at the highest level of training all schools emphasize the cultivation of *Shen* 神 (spirit) in order to refine their skills and connect with the Universal Way. From this spiritual perspective, we call martial arts *WuDao* 武道—the Dao of Nonviolence.

How might one reach this highest level? How does one cultivate *Shen*? To engage in this level of practice we must cultivate our *De* 德. *De* is of fundamental importance in Daoism, so much so that it is found in the title of the Daoist canon, LaoZi's *DaoDeJing* 道德經. Where Dao is the principle of the Universe, *De* is the function, application, and method of following the Dao. *De* means virtue, integrity, and honor. We are virtuous when our actions and behaviors follow the Dao. Traditionally, the primary focus of all martial arts training is the cultivation of *De*. Ideally, the master will not agree to teach a student unless she is sure that the student is a good person. This is one of the reasons the true martial arts master refrains from passing along her entire system of knowledge at one time. As we say in China, *ZhiRenZhiMianBuZhiXin* 知人知面不知心—know the person, know the face, but know not the heart. Special techniques of the lineage are not freely taught because no matter how a student originally presents himself, it takes a considerable length of time until the master is confident that she knows his true heart. The most important quality of any student is the willingness required for a lifetime's work toward becoming *ZhenRen* 真人—a real person. In Chinese, a real person is one who embodies *De* in all aspects of her daily life.

故幾於道　處眾人之所惡　水善利萬物而不爭　上善若水

ShangShanRuoShui ShuiShanLiWanWuErBuZheng
ChuZongRenZhiSuoWu GuJiYuDao[6]

(A person of great virtue is like water
Benefitting all things without asking for reward
Residing where others don't dare
And therefore close to the Dao)

In Daoist internal alchemy and martial arts training we habitually strive to imitate the way of water. We practice our movements slowly and gently to make our bodies supple and yielding. This soft cultivation progressively awakens our consciousness to a level where goodness, compassion, and strength of spirit predominate our thoughts, words, and actions. When in a situation of conflict in our daily life or in face-to-face combat with an opponent, this water quality helps us face the challenges with fearlessness, compassion, and peace.

---

6   LaoZi, *DaoDeJing*, Chapter 8.

III. *DaiShiXinYiLiuHeQuan*
戴氏心意六合拳
Dai Family Heart-Mind Six Unions Martial Arts

The Dao is formless, shapeless, invisible, and intangible. However, it is also carried by anything at any moment. As the opening message of *ZhongYong* 中庸[7] states:

離 | 須 | 不 | 道
也 | 臾 | 可 | 也
　 | 　 | 　 | 者

DaoYeZe BuKe XuYu LiYe

The Dao
Is never apart

Through mindful observation and patient study we can learn about the Dao through any one single thing. In the beginning of traditional Qigong or martial arts training we also focus solely on learning the primary essential element of the school in question, lest we lose ourselves by floating on the surface of many forms without ever coming to truly understand any of them. After we have built up our foundation by mastering one form, it is then easier to learn other forms from different schools well, which allows us to broaden our view of *WuDao*.

Following this tradition, I will not overwhelm you by presenting *WuDao* in relationship to many different forms from many different schools. Instead, I will demonstrate *WuDao* by offering systematic instruction of select internal martial arts practices from one school—*DaiShiXinYiLiuHeQuan* 戴氏心意六合拳 (Dai Family Heart-Mind Six Unions Martial Arts)[8]—to demonstrate *WuDao*. There are three reasons that I have chosen the Dai

---

7 One of the most important Confucian classics; it is commonly held that Confucius' grandson ZiShi (483–402 BCE) wrote the book.

8 I abbreviate the full name of the Dai Family system to "Dai Family XinYi" throughout the majority of this book.

Family XinYi system over the other martial arts systems I have learned to present the Dao of martial arts in this book:

1. Dai Family XinYi holds its roots in *DaoJia YinXianPai* 道家隱仙派 (the Daoist Hidden Immortal Lineage).[9] It is *DanDaoWuShu* 丹道武術— an internal martial arts system entirely based on the principles of Daoist alchemy. Like all traditional Chinese martial arts schools, this system embodies the richness and depth of Daoist philosophy and provides a method to explore healing, internal alchemy, and spiritual transformation.

2. Dai Family XinYi is perhaps the most rare of the martial art forms in China, and for that reason it is a highly treasured school (Over the last 30 years I have dedicated my life to uncovering and studying near-lost Qigong and martial arts forms throughout China.) After many years of great effort, I was fortunate enough to learn of Grandmaster Zhao ShouRong 趙守榮 and, later, even more fortunate to have the opportunity to study Dai Family XinYi with him. It is important to both Grandmaster Zhao and myself to preserve this rare gem and to share this unique system with others committed to exploring classical Chinese martial arts.

3. This book is inspired by my relationship with Grandmaster Zhao and I am happy to have his blessings for this work. He is a great inspiration to me, as he has been practicing Dai Family XinYi for 65 years and has dedicated almost his entire life to preserve this martial arts system and pass it to his students with an open heart. He often urges me to do what I can to make sure the world does not lose this powerful, profound martial arts system. For many years, he has encouraged me to write a book about Dai Family XinYi and to pass the lineage teachings on to my students, regardless of their nationality. In 2011 Grandmaster Zhao and I happily welcomed 26 of my Western students to TaiGu to train daily—several hours a day with myself and several hours a day with Grandmaster Zhao. Many of my students found themselves very inspired that, despite his age, Grandmaster Zhao holds great power and fluidity in his movements. I hope you will enjoy some photos from our trip.

---

9   For details about the Hidden Immortal Lineage, please read Chapter 7 of my book, *Seeking the Spirit of The Book of Change* (2009), also published by Singing Dragon.

In step-by-step fashion, I will share the essential training methods of Dai Family XinYi in this book, including some of the most secret teachings of Dai Family XinYi—the practice of *BaGua XinJing* 八卦心鏡. Until this book, *BaGua XinJing* practice has never been made available to the general public, not even in China. Throughout the book, I will also interpret the connections among Daoist numerology, internal alchemy, healing, and the spirit of classical Chinese martial arts. You will also find a brief description of the martial arts principle behind each movement. (I have focused on the principle behind each movement as opposed to a specific application because in traditional martial arts there is no such thing as a single martial arts application—each movement holds a myriad of applications.)

Disciplined practice of the XinYi martial arts techniques introduced in this book builds strength and stamina and brings one closer to the Dao through a process of inner transformation clearly defined in classical Chinese texts. For those of you who are more visual learners, I will offer instruction of all these movements with some additional martial arts combat demonstrations in my companion XinYi DVD.

Of course, as I always emphasize, the profundity inherent within all classical Qigong and martial arts can only be truly transmitted through *KouChuanXinShou* 口傳心授—(passing with the mouth and transmitting through the heart.) Please look for a qualified teacher to guide your cultivation if you are serious about further exploring the Dai Family XinYi system.

I hope this book will shine a light on the spirituality inherent in classical Chinese martial arts, help bring you into relationship with the authentic force that arises from your *DanTian* 丹田,[10] and fuel your inspiration as you move through life!

Harmonious Qi,

Master Zhongxian Wu   吳忠賢

Autumn is Established, Year of Yin Water Snake   癸巳立秋
Phoenix Nest, Sweden   於瑞典鳳棲巢

---

10 "Elixir Field." There are three *DanTian* in internal alchemy: the upper *DanTian*, located in the third eye; the middle *DanTian*, which is within the center of the chest; and the lower *DanTian*, which resides in the lower belly. Unless otherwise specified, when I mention the *DanTian* I am referring to the lower *DanTian*.

Seeking the root—XinYi China Trip 2011

Grandmaster Zhao guiding group practice

Grandmaster Zhao teaching martial arts applications

Students practicing BengQuan

KouChuanXinShou—Grandmaster Zhao and Master Wu

Master Wu presents his XinYi calligraphy to Grandmaster Zhao

Chapter 1

Dao 道

Daoist Philosophy
and DanWu 丹武

道以立武
武以演道

DaoYiLiWu WuYiYanDao

The Dao generates martial arts
Martial arts display the Dao

XINYI PROVERB
(PASSED THROUGH THE ORAL TRADITION)

1.1 Hen and Egg—The All Too Familiar Conundrum

Daoist philosophy is the fundamental root of traditional Chinese martial arts. The more deeply you understand the Dao, the better your martial arts skills will be. What is the Dao, you may then wonder? Although *DaDaoZhiJian* 大道至簡 (the Great Dao is extremely simple), this is a difficult question to answer. The best place to begin looking for the answer is the first line of LaoZi's *DaoDeJing*:

非	道
常	可
道	道

DaoKeDao FeiChangDao

Literally, this sentence is translated as: "The Dao that can be the Dao is not the constant Dao." It sounds like a maze. With some knowledge of classical Chinese behind you, the translation may be interpreted as follows: "The Dao that can be spoken is not the eternal Dao." Still, however, you may feel confused. After some years of a dedicated inner cultivation practice, I have come to a different interpretation of the sentence: "The Dao, discussed in any language, loses its original meaning." In other words, we cannot truly understand the Dao simply through words alone. As the way to attain the eternal Dao is wordless, the way to access the Dao must be through direct bodily experience. In order to gain this experiential knowledge, you must be seriously committed to your inner cultivation practice. The path to the eternal Dao involves gaining a deep understanding of your physical body, your Qi body, and your spiritual body. This is because the path to the eternal Dao is not mental or verbal—rather, it is experiential.[1]

Behind these words is a powerful teaching encouraging us to use our cultivation practice to connect with the Dao. The Dai Family XinYi internal alchemical martial arts system offers a method of understanding the "wordless teachings" of the Dao by experiencing it through our bodies, our breath,

---

[1] You may read more about this in my article, "LaoZi—Hidden Dragon," *Empty Vessel: A Journal of Daoist Philosophy and Practice*, Winter 2013.

and our spirits. Through this understanding you will also be able to refine your martial arts skills. Some practitioners prefer to study Daoist philosophy before learning martial arts, not wanting to blindly enter into a system of study. Most traditional masters, however, require their students to have at least one year of dedicated practice before exploring the related philosophy. This may be because many people get so lost in the pursuit of understanding through book knowledge that they either never take the action required to commit to a regular practice, or become so distracted by their own mental processes that they can't leave their heads long enough to fully experience the practice in their bodies. So then, where do we begin—with practice or study?

This rather tedious (if not pointless) question traps us in the proverbial "hen and egg" situation. Just as the farmer works with both hens and eggs in his day-to-day life, I suggest that having the philosophical context to enrich your practice is essential to reaching your highest aspirations. (As martial arts (or internal alchemy) practitioners, we need both the "hen"—the Daoist philosophy—and the "egg"—the martial arts forms—in our daily cultivation practice. The flow of this book dictates that I will first focus on the "hen," after which I will then share some nice "eggs" in the subsequent chapters. With that, I can continue to work toward the answer to my beginning question: "What is the Dao?"

The Chinese character 道 (Dao) is simply a trail, road, or path on which to walk. It also means guide, lead, rule, law, way, method, express, speak, justice, and moral. In classical Chinese philosophy, the Dao refers to the way of nature or the universal law. As I discussed in my book *Heavenly Stems and Earthly Branches*, *WenYiZaiDao* 文以載道—(the pattern carries the Dao.[2]) This common saying suggests that the Chinese written characters themselves are vehicles for connecting with nature and channeling universal wisdom. A detailed study of Chinese graphemes, especially of Oracle Script (the oldest-known Chinese written pattern), allows us to garner greater insight from the ancient Chinese sages.

---

2   *Heavenly Stems and Earthly Branches—TianGan DiZhi: The Heart of Chinese Wisdom Traditions* (2014), by Master Zhongxian Wu and Dr. Karin Taylor Wu, also published by Singing Dragon.

Figure 1: Dao in Oracle Script (calligraphy by Master Zhongxian Wu)

In Oracle Script, the Chinese character Dao 道 is composed of three radicals. Xing 行 is an image of an intersection, symbolizing the connection among all energies and all directions, and is the same symbol used for "Element" in Five Elements philosophy. The other two radicals are found sandwiched within Xing itself; found directly in the center of the entire character is Shou 首, a pattern of a head, which symbolizes observe, think, decision, or wisdom; Zhi 止 is a picture of a foot, located at the bottom of the character, which represents walk or action. From the perspective of my cultivation practice, the ancient symbol Dao is a portrait of a high-level martial artist or Qigong master with her feet rooting deeply into the earth, head upright connecting with heaven, and entire body physically and spiritually open and merging with the universe itself. This is an illustration of the supreme state mentioned in all classical Chinese arts—*TianRenHeYi* 天人合一—the oneness between human being and nature.

LaoZi further elucidates the meaning of the Dao for us in Chapter 25 of his *DaoDeJing*:

字之曰道	吾不知其名	可以為天地母	周行而不殆	獨立而不改	寂兮寥兮	先天地生	有物混成

YuWuHunCheng XianTianDiSheng JiXiLiaoXi
DuLiErBuGai ZhouXingErBuDai
KeYiWeiTianDiMu WuBuZhiQiMing ZiZhiYueDao

Something unfathomable created
Birthed before heaven and earth
Within the silence and void
Standing alone and unchanging
Revolving without exhausting
May be the mother of heaven and earth
I do not know her name
I call her Dao

From this description, we can imagine that the Dao is the origin of the primordial universe. In the Daoist classic *QingJingJing* 清靜經, LaoZi describes the Dao as both source and driving force of nature:

大道無形
生育天地

大道無情
運行日月

大道無名
長養萬物

吾不知其名
強名曰道

DaDaoWuXing ShengYüTianDi
DaDaoWuQing YunXingRiYue
DaDaoWuMing ChangYangWanWu
WuBuZhiQiMing QiangMingYueDao

The Great Dao is formless
Gives birth to heaven and earth
The Great Dao is emotionless
Conveys the motion of the sun and the moon
The Great Dao is nameless
Raises and nourishes the Ten-Thousand-Things
I do not know her name
I name her Dao

Try as we may, words (even inspired ones) will eventually fail to express the true nature of the Dao. The only way to experience the reality of the Dao is through our inner cultivation practice. In the next section, I must continue discussing the "hen" in order to explain the Dai Family XinYi system in relation to Daoist philosophy—after which we can begin tasting the "eggs"!

1.2 Digital—The Exciting Reality

Digital technology brings all kinds of magic into our modern lives. The universe has its own mysterious digital system which designs all phenomena in our lives. In Chapter 42 of the *DaoDeJing*, LaoZi applies an easy mathematical pattern to show us how creation of the world relates to the Dao:

道生一　一生二　二生三　三生萬物

DaoShengYi YiShengEr ErShangSan SanShengWanWu

Dao gives birth to one
One gives birth to two
Two gives birth to three
And three gives birth to Ten-Thousand-Things

In this paragraph, LaoZi describes the four evolutionary stages of our universe. Although he did not directly mention zero, in the Daoist numerology system (Zero is used to represent the Dao.) The number 1 represents Chaos, or the primordial state of the universe, which was generated by 0 (the Dao); 2 represents Heaven and Earth (i.e. Yin and Yang), which were generated by 1 (Chaos); and 3 represents the trinity and all new life energy, which was generated by 2 (Heaven and Earth). The Ten-Thousand-Things represent everything in existence, including time and space, and were generated by 3 (the Trinity). These four steps provide the basic blueprint for all *NeiDan* 內丹—internal alchemy—and *DanWu* 丹武—alchemical martial arts practices. Table 1 shows how the Dai Family XinYi system fits into this fundamental model of the universe.

Table 1: Universal Evolution

Stages of evolution	Digital mode	Internal alchemy process	Dai Family XinYi system
1	0 → 1	*LianJingHuaQi* 煉精化炁	*WuJi HunYuan* 無極混元
2	1 → 2	*LianQiHuaShen* 煉炁化神	*Taiji LiangYi* 太極兩儀
3	2 → 3	*LianShenHuanXu* 煉神還虛	*SanCai SiXiang* 三才四象
4	3 → 10,000	*LianXuHeDao* 煉虛合道	*WanQuan GuiZong* 萬拳歸宗

The essence of the entire Dai Family XinYi system begins with mastering the *WuJi HunYuan* 無極混元 standing postures. This practice helps us experience the process of moving from the Dao (0) to primordial Chaos (1). Traditionally, the master will require all novices (students without any foundation in Daoist internal alchemy) to complete *SanNianZhuangGong* 三年椿功 (three years standing GongFu) before moving on to the next level of training. During these three years, the practitioner's sole focus is on the *WuJi HunYuan* standing postures, which we will discuss in detail in Chapter 2. In Chapter 3 we will discuss the second stage of training, *Taiji LiangYi* 太極兩儀—the moving body method, which follows the evolution of 1 giving birth to 2; in Chapter 4 we cover the third stage of training (2 gives birth to 3), the *SanCai SiXiang* 三才四象 stepping technique. I will cover the fourth stage, represented by the 3 giving birth to the Ten-Thousand-Things, in Chapters 5, 6, and 7.

Although *ShuShu* 數術, the art of numbers and calculations, includes the modalities of FengShui, Chinese cosmology, Chinese astrology, Yijing prediction, and Chinese medicine (the higher levels of these traditional arts all involve calculations), for practical purposes this book will focus only on the components of Daoist theory and numerology that relate to internal alchemy and martial arts training.

In the Daoist tradition, numerology itself has two aspects—Yin and Yang. All even numbers represent Yin qualities, whereas odd numbers represent Yang qualities. Within this YinYang designation, the Yang system illustrates external development and the Yin system specifies internal development. With respect to XinYi martial arts, the Yang system focuses on building external force and fighting skills while the Yin system centers on generating inner power.

The two main Daoist classical texts that the serious student will study are the *DaoDeJing* and *YiJing*. Let us first discuss the *DaoDeJing*.

In LaoZi's Hidden Immortal Lineage, we apply *YiQiHuaSanQing* 一炁化三清,[3] or model of the Trinity, to help understand the pattern of external development within the universe. We can use a number system to show this process:

$$1 \text{ transforms to } 3 \rightarrow 3 \times 3 = 9 \rightarrow 9 \times 9 = 81$$

In this arrangement, 1 represents the Dao, 3 represents the Trinity (Heaven, Earth, and human being), 9 represents longevity and/or immortality, and 81 represents the return to the Dao. The *DaoDeJing* is made up of 81 chapters. This external structure follows the Yang numerology system, while the inner content reveals that the *DaoDeJing* is a guide for the internal alchemy practitioner. In the XinYi system, there are 81 forms to help students cultivate their Yang energy and martial power. We use these 81 forms to help us understand the peaceful spirit of martial arts.

In Hidden Immortal Lineage, we use *TaijiShengLiangYi* 太極生兩儀[4] or Duality model to depict the inner driving force of the development of and within the universe. The mathematical pattern below shows this process of generating inner power:

$$1 \times 2 = 2 \rightarrow 2 \times 2 = 4 \rightarrow 4 \times 2 = 8 \rightarrow 8 \times 8 = 64$$

---

3   一炁化三清—"One Qi transforms to Three Purities." According to Daoist mythology, the primordial universe was one mass of Qi. This one mass of Qi transformed to the three Gods of Purity (Supreme Purity, Jade Purity, and Utmost Purity). These three Purities in turn created the world.

4   太極生兩儀—"Taiji Generates Yin and Yang." In the *YiJing*, this principle is used to describe how the Eight Trigrams were created.

In this pattern, 1 symbolizes the Dao, Change, or Taiji; 2 stands for *LiangYi* 兩儀 (Yin and Yang); 4 represents *SiXiang* 四象—the four spiritual animals, four directions, four seasons, and four limbs; 8 symbolizes the *BaGua* 八卦 (Eight Trigrams); and 64 represents the 64 Hexagrams. The *YiJing* has 64 chapters. While this external structure follows the Yin numerology system, the inner content focuses on how to cultivate your Yang energy and emulate the ceaselessness of the Heavenly Way. Like cell division within the body, this pattern is the way of prenatal development and of our process of generating internal energy. Within the YiJing divination system, we must thoroughly learn the symbolism of the *BaGua* before we can begin to learn the 64 Hexagrams. This is the same as Dai Family XinYi martial arts training: the source of power within this Daoist *DanWu* system is hidden within *BaGua XinJing*—eight gentle movements associated with the *BaGua*. While on the surface these movements appear to be very Yin and help to strengthen our internal energies, they also awaken our spiritual gates and help us gain access to the internal driving force of our external power. As you progress in your training, these eight basic movements give rise to 64 advanced practices.

In Table 2 I list the basic numerological relationships, Daoist concepts, and XinYi internal alchemical martial arts practices for you. I hope this provides you with a clear overview of the Dai Family XinYi system.

Table 2: Daoist Numerology and XinYi Practices

Number	Daoist concept	XinYi practice
0	*WuJi* 無極 The Body of the Dao	*WuXing* 無形 Formless
1	*Taiji* 太極 The Function of the Dao	*HunYuan* 混元 Prenatal Standing
2	*LiangYi* 兩儀 Yin and Yang	*LongShen* 龍身 Dragon Body Method
3	*SanCai* 三才 The Trinity	*ChangSanBu* 長三步 Trinity Movement
4	*SiXiang* 四象 Four Spiritual Animals	*SiBa* 四把 Four Movements Form
5	*WuXing* 五形 Five Elements/Phases	*WuXing* 五形拳 Five Elements Form
6	*LiuHe* 六合 Six Unions	*NeiWaiSanHe* 內外三合 Union of Internal and External Trinities
7	*QiXing* 七星 Big Dipper—Heart	*QiPao/QiQuan* 七炮／七拳 Seven Fires/Seven Fists
8	*BaGua* 八卦 Eight Trigrams	*BaXinJing* 八心鏡 Eight Heart Mirrors
9	*JiuGong* 九宮 Nine Palaces	*YuLong JiuGong* 雲龍九宮 Cloudy Dragon Nine Palaces Form
10	*ShiTianGan* 十天干 Ten Heavenly Stems	*ShiDaXing* 十大形 Ten Great Spiritual Animals Form

Chapter 2

WuJi HunYuan 無極混元

The Essence of Daoist Alchemical Martial Arts

合抱之木
生於毫末

HeBaoZhiMu ShengYuHaoMo

The mightiest tree begins as a hair's width sprout

LAOZI 老子

2.1 The Daoist Binary Numbers

In this chapter, I will concentrate on the XinYi practice associated with the numbers 0 and 1. Please take a look around you—it is likely that computers, the Internet, GPS, smart phones, and the digital world play at least some role in your daily life. If it weren't for the discovery of the modern binary number system, we might not have had access to the contemporary thrills of digital technology. However, very few of us know that the discovery of binary numbers was related to Daoist YiJing numerology. Here is a short citation from Wikipedia:

> The modern binary number system was discovered by Gottfried Leibniz in 1679. See his article: *Explication de l'Arithmétique Binaire* (1703). Leibniz's system uses 0 and 1, like the modern binary numeral system. As a Sinophile, Leibniz was aware of the Yijing (or I-Ching) and noted with fascination how its hexagrams correspond to the binary numbers from 0 to 111111, and concluded that this mapping was evidence of major Chinese accomplishments in the sort of philosophical mathematics he admired.[1]

Knowing that the simplest numbers, 0 and 1, were used to create a vastly complex digital world, which continues to impact the course of human existence globally, brings another level of validity to the Daoist numerology system. In Daoist numerology, 0 and 1 created the entire universe and everything in existence. The same holds true within the martial arts system: All different schools, forms, and movements of classical Chinese martial arts are based on these two numbers. This is the reason that all traditional martial arts schools emphasize the importance of spending years focusing on the practice of *JiBenGong* 基本功,[2] the simple, fundamental roots of training. Within the heart of each school's entire system lies its *JiBenGong*. Most of the time (if not always), *JiBenGong* practice appears at first to be rather boring; in order to work directly with the 0 (the Dao), the primary focus is on nothing

---

1 "Binary number," available at http://en.wikipedia.org/wiki/Binary_number, accessed November 4, 2013.

2 *Ji* 基 means foundation, *Ben* 本 means root, and *Gong* 功 means practice, method, and working hard in the correct way. Each traditional Qigong or martial arts school has its own *JiBenGong* which is similar to an entrance exam for the entire system.

more than 1—one single standing posture or movement. Appearances aside, we now know, more than ever, the magic that arises from "just" 0 and 1.

In Daoist numerology, 0 and 1 represent different aspects of the Dao. 0 is often used interchangeably with _WuJi_ 無極, that is, formless chaos, the void, the great silence, and that which is untouchable. _WuJi_ describes _DaoTi_ 道體—the body of the Dao. The number 1 represents _Taiji_ 太極, the driving force of Nature. _Taiji_ also illustrates _DaoYong_ 道用—the function and expression of the Dao that brings all material, events, and phenomena into existence. _DaoYong_ allows us to directly experience the Dao through a palpable awareness born from inner cultivation practices like _NeiDanGong_ 內丹功.[3] Dai Family XinYi is a special type of _NeiDanGong_, study of which begins with _WuJi HunYuan_ 無極混元, the magic numbers 0 and 1.

Are you ready to savor our first "egg"?

---

3   _Nei_ 內 means internal, inner, and inside; _Dan_ 丹 means red, elixir, and alchemy; _Gong_ 功 means practice, method, and working hard in the correct way. _NeiDanGong_ refers to all Daoist internal alchemy cultivations.

2.2 The Foundation—
LianJingHuaQi 煉精化炁
Transforming the Jing to Qi

The foundational practice of the entire XinYi system is *LianJingHuaQi,* an internal alchemy[4] process that embodies the first stage of evolution—the Dao giving birth to 1. Please remember that this is the most important stage of your journey into internal alchemy or XinYi martial arts—it is from here that you build the foundation for everything that is to follow. If you ever feel yourself getting tired of repeating this practice, please remember the following excerpt from Chapter 64 of the *DaoDeJing*:

始於足下｜千里之行｜起於累土｜九層之臺｜生於毫末｜合抱之木

HeBaoZhiMu ShengYuHaoMo JiuCengZhiTai
QiYuLeiTu QianLiZhiXing ShiYuZuXia

The mightiest tree begins as a hair's width sprout
A nine-story dais begins as a single layer of clay
A thousand-mile journey begins as one step

2.2.1 *WuJi Zhuang* 無極椿[5]

Movement: In a standing position, bring your feet together; straighten your body with your head upright and feet rooting into the earth. Relax your shoulders, elbows, and wrists. Feel as though you are standing as relaxed as a pine tree. Continue to adjust your body: your toes grab the earth, tongue touches the upper tooth ridge behind your teeth, tailbone and lower belly are

---

4 This book focuses on the practical aspects of *DanWu*. For more details about the principles of internal alchemy, you can read my books *The 12 Chinese Animals* (2010) and *Chinese Shamanic Cosmic Orbit Qigong* (2011), both published by Singing Dragon.

5 *Wu* 無 (no), *Ji* 極 (polarity, limit), *Zhuang* 椿 (stump). Traditionally, all standing postures are practiced while balanced on tree stumps cut to different heights.

gently tucked, and the perineum is lifted. Keep your teeth and mouth closed. Relax your eyelids.

Breath: Regulate your breathing to be slow, smooth, deep, and even.

Figure 2: WuJi Zhuang

Visualization: Feel your breath gradually melting your physical body and all your thoughts so that your whole being moves into the *WuJi* state— *WuXingWuXiang QuanTiTouKong* 無形無象 全體透空;[6] formless and shapeless, your entire body feels transparent.

Internal Alchemy Principle: This is the practice of *WuJi* or zero (0). *WuJi* describes formless chaos, an early stage of the primordial state, and the practice itself follows the internal alchemy teachings of the *DaoDeJing*

---

6   *Wu* 無 (no), *Xing* 形 (form), *Wu* 無 (no), *Xiang* 象 (pattern), *Quan* 全 (complete, entire), *Ti* 體 (body), *Tou* 透 (penetrate, transparent, connect, flow), *Kong* 空 (void, emptiness).

and *QingJingJing*: *WuWei DanFa* 無為丹法[7]—Actionless Alchemy. From external appearances, it seems you are doing nothing. However, the benefits of this practice are immeasurable. Standing in *WuJi Zhuang* brings stability to your mind, strengthens your physical health, and provides a way for you to connect with the Dao. In martial arts, the standing postures help you achieve the highest state of the practice—*WuXing* 無形, the formless form, which I will discuss in Chapter 7 in this book. You will find a standing posture in all traditional Qigong and martial arts schools.

Figure 3: LongXing Zhuang 龍行樁[8]

---

7   *Wu* 無 (no), *Wei* 為 (action), *Dan* 丹 (elixir), *Fa* 法 (method).
8   Some standing postures are more complicated, like *LongXing Zhuang* 龍行樁, Dragon Standing Posture.

Martial Arts Principle: *XinDingShenNing* 心定神寧[9] is a necessary skill in all traditional martial arts training. With an uneasy heart and nervous spirit, you will have difficulty defeating your competitors even if their skill level is much lower than yours. This practice will help you relax your heart and calm your spirit. The martial arts principle is known as *DingFa* 定瀘—The Method of Tranquility.

After at least a few minutes (or hours) of *WuJi Zhuang* practice we can move to the next posture.

2.2.2 HunYuan Zhuang 混元椿

Movement: From the *WuJi* posture, bend your knees slightly, tuck in your tailbone, and tighten your bottom muscles. Curve your back and close your shoulders by bringing them close together in front of your body and sucking in your chest. Do not stick your bottom out! Bring your forearms and hands together in front of your body (the pinky edges of your hands are together) with your palms facing forward. The backs of your hands rest on your thighs as you hold your arms as close to your body as you can. Keep your head upright with eyesight horizontal.

This posture is also known as *DunMaoHou* 蹲貓猴, which literally means squatting cat-monkey, because while in it, the practitioner resembles a squatting cat or monkey. In truth, there are six spiritual animals contained within this posture. When you hold this posture, align yourself with the six spiritual animals (described below) through your breathing and visualization techniques.

Breath: With each breath, breathe with your lungs, your skin, and your navel. With each inhalation, imagine all the pores of your skin are open and allow the universal Qi, like sunlight, to enter into your body and gather at your navel. With each exhalation, imagine the Qi descending from your navel to your *DanTian* 丹田 (the elixir field in your lower belly).

---

9   *Xin* 心 (heart), *Ding* 定 (stable, calm), *Shen* 神 (spirit), *Ning* 寧 (calm, tranquil)—concentrating the Heart-Mind and calming the spirit.

Figure 4: HunYuan Zhuang front view

Figure 5: HunYuan Zhuang side view

Visualization:

- *JiTui* 雞腿—**Rooster Leg:** When you are standing in this posture, imagine a rooster standing in the cold on one leg and tucking the other leg all the way up to snug his belly. Feel the power of the one rooster claw that is bearing the weight of his entire body. The rooster claw is a symbol for martial power. Your toes are your own "rooster claws." Use force as you grab the floor with your toes, holding the posture as the rooster stands on one leg. Keep your knees and legs together such that your two legs merge into one. It is very important to remember your alignment—*never* bend your knees so much that they extend beyond your toes.

  Another name for this leg posture is *HanJi Tui* 寒雞腿, which literally means cold-rooster leg. Traditionally, martial arts are taught surreptitiously and the name of a movement or posture often carries deeper, hidden messages. *HanJi* 寒雞 does not merely mean cold rooster, it actually suggests another phrase, *HanJi* 含機, which means hidden trigger, as in a trigger for a secret trap. While standing in this posture, you can secretly shift your weight to one leg while you use the other to kick your opponent.

- *XiongYao* 熊腰—**Bear Waist:** Bring the image of a bear to your mind when you check your waist while maintaining this standing posture. The bear has a sloped bottom and powerful waist. Make sure to tuck your tailbone in and wrap the buttock muscles tightly, holding the energy in and containing it within the *DanTian*. This animal imagery helps remind you during your martial arts practice that the strong powerful bear-like energy in your waist is generated from the *DanTian*.

- *HouBei* 猴背—**Monkey Back:** During your standing, also picture a monkey sitting on a rock and enjoying the sunshine as you curve your back. In the internal alchemy tradition, the monkey represents spirituality. When you make the monkey back, you work directly with your spine, the spiritual channel of the body, and awaken your spiritual energy.

- *YingBang* 鷹膀—**Eagle Shoulders:** Envision an eagle standing on top of a tree with his wings totally closed and folded in close to his body when you close your shoulders. The eagle represents the spirit of the heart and, in internal alchemy, the shoulders are symbolically related to the heart. This aspect of the practice helps strengthen the physical function of the heart and is also good for the shoulders.

- *HuBaoTou* 虎豹頭—**Tiger-Leopard Head:** See the tiger and leopard stalking their prey as you keep your eyes alert and head upright. These two magnificent and powerful beasts represent your awakened consciousness.

Internal Alchemy Principle: This is the practice of *HunYuan* 混元 (Oneness, and the number 1 itself). *Hun* 混 means mix, turbid, and unclear; *Yuan* 元 means origin and source. Together, *HunYuan* is the term for the middle stage of primordial chaos—One Qi, the pre-state of Taiji when there is still no separation between Yin and Yang. This standing posture is the most important posture for the entire Dai Family XinYi system. Just like the 1 (*DaoYong*, the function of the Dao) that carries everything, this posture holds the key elements for every form and movement within the XinYi school. If you do not have this posture, all your other movements will be without foundation.

The process of internal alchemy cultivation is *FanHuangZhiDao* 返還之道[10]—the way of returning to the source. This posture helps us move back to the prenatal state. In it, we imitate the fetal curve of the baby in utero. In the prenatal state, we were all residing in the cave of our mother's womb, focusing on our own development and not being distracted by the external world. After birth, in the postnatal state, we habitually focus more and more on the external world, which causes us to lose connection with our *ShenQi* 神炁, our spiritual energy. The cultivation practice helps bring our minds back to our body, awaken our Jing 精 (essence), Qi 炁 (vital energy), and Shen 神 (spirit), heighten our awareness of Qi, and strengthen the flow of Qi in our meridian systems (especially the conception and governing meridians). When you practice this posture, feel that you are returning to the fetal state and breathe into your *DanTian*.

---

10 *Fan* 返 (reverse), *Huang* 還 (return), *Zhi* 之 (of), *Dao* 道 (the way).

Martial Arts Principle: In *DanWu*, the internal alchemical martial arts system, martial power is derived from the *DanTian*. This fundamental standing posture will help us build up strong Qi in our *DanTian* and learn how to use the power of our *DanTian* Qi throughout the entire body. With committed practice, this spirit within this posture will bring out the function of all other Dai Family XinYi forms—especially during combat. This martial arts principle is called *GuiFa* 歸瀘—The Method of Returning.

2.2.3 *LianJingHuaQiJue* 煉精化炁訣
Transforming the Jing to Qi

眼視鼻　鼻對臍　處處行注不可移　澈二六　連環鎖　一點靈光吊在眉

YanShiBi BiDuiQi ChuChuXingZhuBuKeYi
CheErLiu LianHuanSuo YiDianLingGuangDiaoZaiMei

Eyes observe the nose
Nose aligns to the navel
Pouring attention everywhere without distraction
Awakening within Two–Six
Linking locks
Spiritual light emerges between your eyebrows

This is the Dai Family XinYi internal alchemy meditation poem, which provides precise guidance on how to transform our Jing to Qi. To help you deepen your understanding of the *HunYuan Zhuang* practice, I will provide some commentary on the internal alchemy poem for you below:

YanShiBi 眼視鼻
Eyes observe the nose

In internal alchemy and martial arts practice, the secret trigger for your practice resides in your eyes. It is essential that you bring your eyesight—your spiritual light—back to your body during practice. To do so, relax your eyelids, allowing them to hang down naturally over your eyes, leaving a small slit so that you can almost see the tip of your nose.

Figure 6: Oracle Script for "self"

Why do the eyes observe the nose? In China, the nose has been used to represent the self for thousands of years. The Oracle Script for "self" (Figure 6) is, in fact, the image of a person's nose. In China, if we are in conversation and need to make a gesture indicating self, we point to our nose (as opposed to tapping to the chest as people will do in the West). The nose is the second key element in your practice because it is the primary gateway of accessing heavenly Qi (through the breath). Heaven nourishes human beings by providing the *WuQi* 五氣 (Five Qi) through the nose just as Earth feeds the human being by providing the *WuWei* 五味 (Five Flavors) through the mouth. Through the breath you will be able to calm your mind and bring your consciousness back to your body.

BiDuiQi 鼻對臍
Nose aligns to the navel

During this practice it is important to connect our breathing to our navel. In the fetus, the navel is the gateway to the life source. In your internal alchemy practice, learning to breathe through your navel will help you enter into your prenatal state and re-connect with your vitality.

ChuChuXingZhuBuKeYi 處處行注不可移
Pouring attention everywhere without distraction

It is through your *DanTian* that you are able to gain awareness of every place in your body. Once Jing transforms to Qi, the Qi will naturally move to different areas of your body. In the earlier stages of self-cultivation, Qi-sensations are new to everyone and may feel exciting, scary, or strange. Please remember to stay calm, relaxed, and centered, remembering to stay focused on your breath instead of being distracted by whichever Qi phenomenon is manifesting itself. Do not shift your attention from observing your *DanTian*, your body, and the practice itself—do not lose yourself in sensation or imagination. During your cultivation practice, allow no distractions from the external world or inner phenomena.

CheErLiu 澈二六
Awakening within Two–Six

The guidance laid out for us in the first half of this poem does not only apply to the *WuJi HunYuan* practice. Rather, it is internal alchemy guidance for daily living—look within, pay attention to your breath, and pay attention to your *DanTian* at all times, or at least anytime you are not in your sleeping state. In Chinese tradition, we use the six Yin Earthly Branches and six Yang Earthly Branches to count the 24 hours of a day.[11] Therefore, in traditional Chinese literature, Two–Six is akin to "24/7," or all the time.

LianHuanSuo 連環鎖
Linking locks

This verse reveals how beneficial the results of your cultivation practice can be. Instead of using the word "chain," Chinese use the phrase "locks locking each other" when describing something unbroken or continuous. The Qi circulates within the different meridians of our body. This internal alchemy guidance helps us to generate an ideal, unobstructed flow of Qi in our body.

---

11 In the Chinese clock, there are 12 two-hour segments in each day.

YiDianLinGuangDiaoZaiMei 一點靈光吊在眉
Spiritual light emerges between your eyebrows

The final line of this poem explains the ultimate outcome of deep Qi transformation. In internal alchemy, the upper *DanTian* is located at the center point between your eyebrows (it is also referred to as the third eye). With practice, you will be able to see Qi—like flashes of lightning—shining on and illuminating your way.

Chapter 3

Taiji LianYi 太極兩儀
The Secret of Dragon Body

神龍見尾　不見首

ShenLongXianWei BuXianShou

Mystical dragon shows only its tail
And never reveals its head

CHINESE PROVERB

In this chapter, we will study *LianQiHuaShen* 煉炁化神 (transform the Qi to nourish the spirit), the internal alchemy process of one giving birth to two.

3.1 *LongShen* 龍身
Dragon Body

Once we become proficient in *HunYuan Zhuang* (Chapter 2) we come to a place where we truly integrate the six spiritual animals within the body. Once we become skilled at merging the six into one, we are ready to practice *LongShen* 龍身, the Dragon Body. In Chinese culture, the dragon represents shifting, changing, invisible, mystery, flexibility, transformation, high spirituality, supernatural, and power. We say that no one really knows what dragons look like because they remain hidden in the clouds, never revealing their true face. The Dragon Body practice is a way to express all the characteristics of the dragon in your martial arts practice. *LongShen* is the spirit of the entire Dai Family XinYi system. *LongShen* is possible only through mastery of *HunYuan Zhuang*. All forms that follow are possible only through mastery of *LongShen*. Like a hidden dragon, the Dai Family has held this aspect of the XinYi secret for a long time:

ZhiZhiDaiJia QuanDaRen BuJianDaiJia RenLianQuan

We all know Dai Family martial artists defeat others
Yet there is seldom chance to see them practice!

A high-level Dai Family XinYi master becomes so alive with dragon energy that people have a very hard time predicting what she will do next. In combat, the master will be able to defeat you the moment you blink, without you even being able to realize how she did it.

LongShen works with the movement of Yin and Yang energies. When Yin and Yang move toward each other and interact as one dynamic balanced state, the balanced cooperation is called Taiji 太極. When Yin and Yang move apart from each other, expressing their opposing qualities, we refer to the apparent dualism as *LiangYi* 兩儀.[1]

YinYi 陰儀 (Yin Expression) is a term describing the features of Yin: earth, mother, feminine, darkness, nighttime, unknown, stable, rest, store, recover, preserving your energy, nourish, restore, conserve, internal, introvert, detached, calm, inhale, etc. Yin is the source and reservoir of our life energy and wisdom.

YangYi 陽儀 (Yang Expression) illustrates the qualities of Yang: heaven, father, masculine, brightness, daytime, clear, movement, activity, consume, expending your energy, develop, external, extrovert, desire, eager, exhale, etc. Yang is the power of our life energy, and the potential to show our talents off to the world.

The Dao can be defined as Yin embracing Yang. Daoist cultivation practices focus on bringing Yang energy within Yin and help us move closer to the Dao. While the momentum of life moves us from the prenatal to the postnatal, from Yin to Yang, the momentum of the Dao is the reverse way. The reverse way is the pathway to return to the prenatal state. Guided by this YinYang principle, there are two movements in the *LongShen* practice, *Su* 縮 and *Zhan* 展. *Su* is the movement of Yin expression, whilst *Zhan* is the movement of Yang expression. *LongShen SuZhan* is the secret body method[2] of the Dai Family XinYi system and is the martial arts expression of *LianYi* in your body.

---

1   *Liang* 兩 (two), *Yi* 儀 (expressions).
2   Although *Shen* 身 (body) *Fa* 灋 (method) is an essential component of all martial arts practices, it is the technique most often withheld from the beginner, especially when the master has not yet had enough time to determine the *De* (virtue) of her student.

3.2 *QianLongZaiYuan* 潛龍在淵
Dragon Hidden within the Abyss

Figure 7:
WuJi Zhuang

Figure 8:
Taiji Zhuang

Figure 9: HunYuan Zhuang

Movement: From *WuJi Zhuang* (section 2.2.1), bring hands together, right inside left, and gently touch your lower belly (*DanTian*), to come into *Taiji Zhuang* (see Figure 8). From *Taiji Zhuang*, we will move into *HunYuan Zhuang* (section 2.2.2). Entering into *HunYuan Zhuang* from *Taiji Zhuang* is the *Su* practice and is also called *SuShu* 縮束. *Su* literally means condense, compress, and coil. *Shu* means tie together, bound, bundle, and tight. Move very slowly from *Taiji Zhuang* to *HunYuan Zhuang*: Bend your knees slightly, tuck your tailbone in, and tighten your bottom muscles. Curve your back and close your shoulders by bringing them close together in front of your body and sucking in your chest. Bring your forearms and hands together in front of your body (the pinky edges of your hands are together) with your palms facing forward. The backs of your hands rest on your thighs as you hold your arms as close to your body as you can. Keep your head upright with eyesight horizontal. Perform this movement very slowly at first, speeding up only once you feel very comfortable with your ability to remember all the details of the movement.

Breath: Inhale, taking the universal Qi in through all the pores of your skin, through your navel and into your *DanTian*.

Visualization: Imagine your body is coiled like a dragon and sinking into the bottom of a great abyss. At the same time, feel each of your Three Hearts—*DingXin* 頂心 (the heart of your head, located at *BaiHui* 百會 [also known as GV20], an important acupuncture point on the top of your head), *ShouXin* 手心 (the heart of your hand, which is found on *LaoGong* 勞宮 [the acupuncture point known as PC8], located in the central area of your palm), and *ZuXin* 足心 (the heart of your foot, also known as *YongQuan* 湧泉 or KD1, which lies in the center of the ball of your foot)—connecting to your *DanTian*.

Internal Alchemy Principle: This movement is a way to open the conception meridian and strengthen your *DanTian* Qi. The conception meridian is in charge of all the Yin meridians of your body and it generates and nourishes Yang Qi/life energy. There is a saying in traditional internal alchemy practice:

任　百
脈　病
通　消

RenMaiTong BaiBingXiao

Conception meridian flowing
A hundred diseases dismissed!

This practice has very powerful healing functions. Curving your body and condensing your energy within your *DanTian* is an internal alchemy method known as *FanBenHuanYuan* 返本還原,[3] which allows us to return to the state of our original essence—the prenatal body. Please remember that this practice emphasizes breathing through the skin and navel down to the *DanTian*.

Martial Arts Principle: In the Dai Family XinYi system, we never encourage going directly against your opponent's force during combat. Instead, we emphasize taking in the oncoming force and letting your enemy become trapped in your invisible cage. This practice helps you work on drawing the energy of your opponent in. This martial arts principle is known as *TunFa* 吞灔—The Method of Drawing In.

---

3   *Fan* 返 (return), *Ben* 本 (root), *Huan* 還 (return), *Yuan* 原 (source).

3.3 *FeiLongZaiTian* 飛龍在天
Flying Dragon in the Sky

Movement: Starting from *HunYuan Zhuang*, slowly straighten your body and turn your hands so that your palms touch your lower belly and you are once again in *Taiji Zhuang*. This is the uncurling movement of *Zhan*, which is also called *ShuZhan* 舒展. *Shu* means comfortable, relax, calm, cozy, and open; *Zhan* means expand, stretch, exhibition, and display. As you straighten your body, grab the floor with your toes with continued force, lift and tighten your perineum, keep your teeth and mouth closed, and feel the pressure on the top of your head as you ascend. In this posture, your body is *DingTianLiDi* 頂天立地—pushing up heaven whilst rooting deep into the earth. Make sure to practice this movement slowly for several months before you gradually increase your speed.

Breath: Exhale, allowing the Qi from your *DanTian* to fill up your entire body.

Visualization: Imagine your body is like a dragon leaping out of the abyss and soaring into the sky as you straighten your body. Feel taut and powerful in your Three Hearts as your body expands with Qi.

Internal Alchemy Principle: This practice is a way to strengthen your Yang Qi and the governing meridian, which governs all of the Yang meridians in your body. In internal alchemy, the governing meridian is the ocean of Yang Qi. If the Qi is free flowing within your governing meridian, the Yang Qi will transform into a higher quality of energy that then nourishes and uplifts your spirit.

Practiced together, *SuShu ShuZhan* strengthens the vital link between the governing meridian and conception meridian. This is one of the most important *ZhouTian* 周天 (Cosmic Orbit) methods to transform your Qi and nourish your spirit. In the next section, I will share the Dai Family XinYi *ZhouTian* poem, *LianQiHuan ShenJue*, to help you deepen your practice of the Dragon Body.

Martial Arts Principle: A skillful XinYi master can push her antagonist away with the power of her *DanTian*. This practice helps us to learn how to use our *DanTian* Qi to drive the movement of our body. This martial arts principle is called *TuFa* 吐瀘—The Method of Spitting Out.

Figure 10: HunYuan Zhuang

Figure 11: Taiji Zhuang

3.4 *LianQiHuaShenJue* 煉炁化神訣
Transforming the Qi to Nourish the Spirit

緊攝谷道內中提
尾閭一起皺節骨
玉枕難過目視鼎
來到丹田存消息
往前又是鵲橋路
十二時中降下池
鎖住心猿拴意馬
要到丹田海底基
一時快樂無窮盡
返本還原心自知
久煉自成金剛體
百病皆除如童子

JinSheGuDaoNeiZhongTi

WeiLüYiQiZhouJieGu

YüZhenNanGuoMuShiDing

LaiDaoDanTianCunXiaoXi

WangQianYouShiQueQiaoLu

ShiErShiZhongJiangXiaChi

SuoZhuXinYuanShuanYiMa

YaoDaoDanTianHaiDiJi

YiShiKuaiLeWuQiongJin

FanBenHuanYuanXinZiZhi

JiuLianZiChengJinGangTi

BaiBingJieChuRuTongZi

Tightly close the Valley Path, lift internally

Tuck the tailbone, vertebrae curl

With difficulties passing the Jade-Pillow, observe the Cauldron

Come to the *DanTian*, store the Change

Keep moving forward to the Magpie-Bridge

Always diving into the Pond

Holding the Heart-Ape stable and harnessing the Mind-Horse

Explore the *DanTian* and the Ocean floor

Suddenly, there is infinite joy

The heart knows the prenatal state

With dedicated practice, create the Diamond-Body

Once the hundred-diseases disappear, you emerge as a virgin

JinSheGuDaoNeiZhongTi 緊攝谷道內中提
Tightly close the Valley Path, lift internally

This verse relays a fundamental rule of internal alchemical transformation. *GuDao* 谷道 (Valley Path) is an internal alchemy term for anus. *Gu* is a symbol for life energy. Generally, people are unaware that they constantly leak their life energy through their anus. In traditional Qigong and martial arts practice, one of the first exercises is learning to hold the anus tightly closed, especially during important stages of Qi transformation. Working with *GuDao* in this way helps you contain your life energy so that you may work with *GuShen* 谷神 (Valley Spirit, the source of your life). In Chapter 6 of the *DaoDeJing*, LaoZi describes this for us:

谷神不死
是謂玄牝
玄牝之門
是謂天地之根

GuShenBuShi
ShiWeiXuanPin
XuanPinZhiMen
ShiWeiTianDiZhiGen

The immortality of the Valley Spirit
Is named the Great Mystery
The gate of the Great Mystery
Is called the Root of Heaven and Earth

Therefore, during your *LongShen* practice, please remember to lift your anus and close it firmly with a strong inner force.

WeiLüYiQiZhouJieGu 尾閭一起皺節骨
Tuck the tailbone, vertebrae curl

Here we are given guidance for our *Su* practice and an important juncture in the process of Qi transformation. During *LianQiHuaShen*, *WeiLü* (the tailbone) is the first gate that the Qi needs to pass through on its way to nourish the *Shen*, which resides in *NiWanGong* 泥丸宮, the Clay Pill Palace (pineal gland). In *Su* practice, we first tuck the tailbone toward the *DanTian*, which then makes it easier to work with curling your vertebrae into the Monkey Back. Your *DanTian* Qi will build up enough strength to move and open the first gate.

YüZhenNanGuoMuShiDing 玉枕難過目視鼎
With difficulties passing the Jade-Pillow, observe the Cauldron

The *YüZhen* (Jade-Pillow) is located at the top of the cervical spinal curve, near the base of your skull. This is the last gate to pass through before the Qi enters the brain so that it may nourish your *Shen* (spirit). The Jade-Pillow is also the most difficult gate for the Qi to pass through. As the Qi gathers here, it is common to feel discomfort in the area if the Qi is unable to push through this gate. It is essential that you do not use your mind to force this gate open if you experience this unpleasant feeling. Instead, simply pay attention to your Cauldron—the internal alchemy symbol for the *DanTian*. The *DanTian* is the source of your energy. Once you have built up enough energy in your *DanTian*, the Qi will move naturally, without effort or exertion, to open the gate at the Jade-Pillow.

LaiDaoDanTianCunXiaoXi 來到丹田存消息
Come to the DanTian, store the Change

As you concentrate your mind on your *DanTian*, you will notice that the Qi will constantly change its quality. You will likely have many sensations occurring throughout your body. *XiaoXi* 消息 means news, waxing–waning, and changing energy. Do not be distracted by these phenomena! Instead keep breathing into your *DanTian*, storing your ever-changing Qi, and waiting for the news that your Qi is strong enough to move and open the Jade-Pillow.

WangQian YouShiQueQiaoLu 往前又是鵲橋路
Keep moving forward to the Magpie-Bridge

After the Qi passes through the Jade-Pillow and nourishes the *Shen*, it will continue moving forward, around to the front of your head. At this point you must remember the Magpie-Bridge, the next juncture the Qi will need to flow through. To build the Magpie-Bridge, keep your tongue touching the upper tooth ridge behind your teeth. In Chinese mythology there is a story of innumerable magpies that used their bodies to form a bridge spanning from earth to heaven. The magpies built the bridge one time each year in order to give a humble cow-herder a chance to see his wife, who was a daughter of the Jade Emperor (the Lord of Heaven). The Magpie-Bridge is a symbol of connecting with the immortals' world—without this method you will not be able to complete this essential stage of internal transformation.

ShiErShiZhongJiangXiaChi 十二時中降下池
Always diving into the Pond

ShiErShi[4] means at all times, and the Pond is the area in your mouth right under your tongue. Once the Qi passes through the Magpie-Bridge, you will feel a build up of saliva as it collects under your tongue. There will also be a strong sensation of Qi pouring through the Magpie-Bridge and into the Pond. Traditionally, saliva is called *ChangShengJiu* 長生酒—"longevity wine"—and it is associated with strong life energy. Once you learn the techniques of *LongShen*, please try implementing them into your daily rhythms. If you can remember to build the Magpie-Bridge and feel the Qi diving into the Pond while you move about in your life, you will be constantly generating your longevity wine. As its name suggests, longevity wine is regarded as a necessary ingredient of a long, healthy life.

SuoZhuXinYuanShuanYiMa 鎖住心猿拴意馬
Holding the Heart-Ape stable and harnessing the Mind-Horse

In traditional Chinese culture, the ape is used to represent the spirit and the horse to represent the mind and thoughts. This verse gives us further instruction about our daily cultivation. Day-to-day realities bring many things that can disturb our practice and destroy our *Shen*. We work to keep our spirit and mind stable with awareness of our breath and of our body so that, no matter what happens, we are not disturbed by the external world. This is the most important principle of nourishing *Shen* and is also the spirit of XinYi (Heart-Mind) internal martial arts.

---

4   *Shi* 十 (ten), *Er* 二 (two), *Shi* 時 (hour, time). Ten and two make twelve. In the Chinese clock, there are 12 two-hour segments in a day. This traditional phrase is used in China as "24/7" is used in the West.

YaoDaoDanTianHaiDiJi 要到丹田海底基
Explore the DanTian and the Ocean floor

In the body, *HaiDiJi* 海底基, the bottom-most surface of the Ocean, is found within the perineum, at *HuiYin* 會陰 (the acupuncture point known as CV1). According to the YinYang principle, Yin gives birth to and nourishes Yang. Your heart and mind have predominantly Yang qualities, always seeking and grasping things in the external world. In order to bring your heart and mind within your body, you need to pay close attention to your *DanTian* as well as your *HaiDiJi*. *HaiDiJi* is the point of the body with the strongest Yin energy. Learning to use this abundance of Yin energy to nourish your constantly depleted Yang will help you hold your Yang energy within. After you reach the level where you feel heat in your *DanTian*, take advantage of the powerful Yin quality of the *Su* practice by breathing into your *HaiDiJi*.

YiShiKuaiLeWuQiongJin 一時快樂無窮盡
Suddenly, there is infinite joy

As you continue breathing into your *HaiDiJi*, you will gain sudden awareness of a natural rush of new Yang or life energy being generated. This will feel like a wonderful surprise and is a source of great internal joy. This surge of Yang energy will deeply nourish your *Shen*.

FanBenHuanYuanXinZiZhi 返本還原心自知
The heart knows the prenatal state

Deeply nourished *Shen* allows you to experience the quiet bliss of the prenatal state. It is something sensed and felt through your own heart. There is really no way to describe it justly through words.

JiuLianZiChengJinGangTi 久煉自成金剛體
With dedicated practice, create the Diamond-Body

The diamond is one of the most stable and enduring materials of the physical world. The qualities of *JinGangTi* 金剛體—the Diamond-Body—are the same—healthy, strong, and everlasting. With a daily, dedicated *LongShen* practice, you will be able to achieve *JinGangTi*.

BaiBingJieChuRuTongZi 百病皆除如童子
Once the hundred-diseases disappear, you emerge as a virgin

In the Daoist tradition, a virgin is a symbol of pure, strong, new life energy. No matter what illness or weaknesses you may have when you begin, the resounding benefit of your martial arts practice is developing strong physical, emotional, and spiritual health. Recovering the purity of your mind and body is a natural result of daily cultivation practice.

Chapter 4

SanCai SiXiang 三才四象
The Way of Circle and Square

知 智
地 天
者 者
智 聖

ZhiDiZheZhi ZhiTianZheSheng

A person who knows the earth is wise
A person who knows heaven is a sage

ZHOUBISUANJING 周髀算經[1]

---

1   *Zhou* 周 (Zhou Dynasty, circular, Heavenly Way), *Bi* 髀 (pointer of a sundial), *Suan* 算 (calculate), *Jing* 經 (classical text). The *ZhouBiSuanJing* is a Chinese astronomy and mathematics text and is reputed to have been written during the Western Zhou Dynasty (1027–771 BCE).

To work with the third stage of our *LiangShenHuanXu* 煉神還虛 (refine the spirit and return to the void) cultivation practice—two gives birth to three—we use the *ChangSanBu* 長三步 (Long Trinity Step) method.

4.1 *YuanFang* 圓方
The Circle and Square

According to Daoist numerology, in the third stage of the evolution, in which two gives birth to three, the number three represents creation, accomplishment, the beginning of postnatal life, and *SanCai*. *SanCai* literally means three materials or three within one. With respect to Daoist philosophy it means trinity—every object, phenomenon, or event in the universe is the sum of three parts. Each of these components is also made of three components (subcomponents, if you will), ad infinitum. *SanCai* as a philosophy explains the mathematical pattern discussed in section 1.2 ($1 \times 3 = 3 \rightarrow 3 \times 3 = 9 \rightarrow 9 \times 9 = 81$). The diagram below provides a conceptual example:

Oneness (Dao, Taiji, or Universe)	→	Heaven	→	Sun
				Stars
				Moon
		Human being	→	Shen
				Qi
				Jing
		Earth	→	Fire
				Wind
				Water

In the Dai Family XinYi system, understanding the trinities within your body is a must, especially the components and subcomponents listed for you in Table 3.

Table 3: Trinity of the Body

Energy trinity	Body trinity	Head trinity	Middle body trinity	Leg trinity	Arm trinity
Shen	Upper/Head	Forehead	Chest	Hip	Shoulder
Qi	Middle	Nose	Upper belly	Knee	Elbow
Jing	Lower/Leg	Jaw	Lower belly	Foot	Wrist

As mentioned, *SanCai* represents any and every thing that exists in the universe. *SanCai* carries the Heavenly Way, which is *Yuan* 圓—circle or circular. In our martial arts practice, we come to understand the ceaseless nature of the Heavenly Way through the uninterrupted flow of energy in our body and through the circular pattern of the movements themselves. Each *SanCai* also has at least one associated *SiXiang* 四象. *SiXiang* literally means four images, and can symbolize the four spiritual animals, four directions, four seasons, four sides of an object, four corners of a square or rectangle, four limbs, etc. *SiXiang* also stands for stability and carries the Earthly Way, which is *Fang* 方—square, rectangle, rectangular, cornered, direction, method, or stability. We come to understand the strength and steadiness of the Earthly Way by practicing the standing postures and by learning to use the *SiShao* 四稍—the Four Tips—of our body (Hair is the tip of blood; Tongue is the tip of muscle; Teeth are the tip of bone; Nails are the tip of tendon) in all of our movements.

Learning to apply the *SanCai SiXiang* concept to our practice helps us to understand Daoist numerology and martial arts skills. The *ZhouBiSuanJing* 周髀算經 states, "*ShuZhiFaChuYuYuanFang* 數之灋出於圓方"—The way of numbers (numerology) emerges from the circle and the square. In the third century, renowned astronomer Zhao Shuang 趙爽 explained the meanings of circle and square: "The circle and square are the shapes of heaven and earth, and embody the numbers of yin and yang."[2] The *ZhouBiSuanJing* also discusses how ancient Chinese astronomers used a simple geometric pattern, the right-angled triangle, as a tool to learn the way of heaven and earth and create the Chinese calendar. As shown in Figure 12, the vertical line of the right-angled triangle, called *Bi* 髀 or *Gu* 股 (which literally means leg and was also the original name for the staff of a sundial), represents heaven; the

---

2   Cullen, Christopher. *Astronomy and Mathematics in Ancient China (ZhouBiSuanJing)*. Cambridge: Cambridge University Press, 1996, p.83.

horizontal line, called *Gou* 勾 (which is the name of the shadow cast by *Bi*), symbolizes earth; and the long oblique line, called *Xuan* 玄, represents both the mystery of nature and human being. In the Daoist tradition, we use the right-angled triangle to represent *SanCai* or the Heavenly Way.

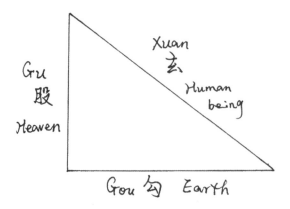

Figure 12: Trinity of the right-angled triangle diagram

A right-angled triangle conveys both *Yuan* and *Fang*. How? All triangles are cyclic, meaning they have associated inscribed and circumscribed circles, and can thus be interpreted as transmitting the Heavenly Way. If we add another right-angled triangle by flipping the first 180 degrees on its hypotenuse (adding mirror *Gou* and *Gu* line images), a rectangle, the carrier of the Earthly Way, is created. *ChangSanBu*—the Long Trinity Step—uses the principles of ancient geometry to help us to embody the Heavenly and Earthly Way.

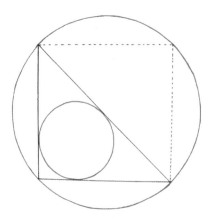

Figure 13: YuanFang of the right-angled triangle diagram

4.2 *ChangSanBu* 長三步
Long Trinity Step

Movement: Starting from *Taiji Zhuang*, use the *Su* method, as discussed in section 3.2, to curve your body while simultaneously pivoting your left foot about 30 degrees to the left and swinging your right foot forward so that your right heel makes contact with the floor and the right knee is locked. This is the *Su* posture of *ChangSanBu*.

Figure 14: ChangSanBu Su front view

Figure 15: ChangSanBu Su side view

In this posture, your body forms energetic circles, squares, and hidden triangles:

Figure 16: Circles, squares, and triangles of ChangSanBu Su

Next, stretch your body into the *Zhan* method I discussed in section 3.3, while moving your right foot forward as far as possible, and turn your right foot 30 degrees to the left so that you stand with both feet perfectly parallel to one another. At the same time turn your palms, right hand inside, to face your *DanTian*. Your left foot does not change position from the previous movement. This is the *Zhan* posture of *ChangSanBu*.

Figure 17: ChangSanBu Zhan

In this posture, your body creates a right-angled triangle:

1. The hypotenuse is the straight line connecting the Heavenly Gate to the Earthly Door.

2. The perpendicular line is created by aligning the tip of the nose tip, tip of knee, and toes (or KD1).

3. The horizontal line is created by the step itself.

Your body has now formed a perfect right-angled triangle, complete with hidden energetic circles and squares, as indicated in Figure 18.

Figure 18: Circles, squares, and triangles of ChangSanBu Zhan

Next, repeat the above step, starting with your right foot turned 30 degrees to the right and moving the left foot forward. Continue practicing the *ChangSanBu* on both sides.

As you begin your practice, please move slowly and gently. After several months, once you are comfortable with the movement and confident that you have the correct alignment, you can speed up and add inner force to the step. With time you will feel your *DanTian* Qi growing strong and your body will feel full of vitality. Finally, you will be able to practice as fast as you can and still feel very light. This is the trinity method of the Dai Family school, as described in LaoZi's *DaoDeJing* (Chapter 25), and can be applied to the entire XinYi system:

RenFaDi DiFaTian TianFaDao DaoFaZhiRan

Human being follows the Earthly Way
The Earthly Way follows the Heavenly Way
The Heavenly follows the Dao
The Dao follows its natural way

Breath: Inhale as you form the *Su* posture and exhale as you come into the *Zhan* posture.

Visualization: Imagine yourself as a crouching tiger leaping out of its cave.

Internal Alchemy Principle: Most of the moving forms of the Dai Family XinYi system are based on the *ChangSanBu* technique. *Chang* means long, stretching, grown, unbroken, longevity, and long life; *San* means three or trinity; and *Bu* means step. This constitutes the third stage in internal alchemy training, *LianShenHuanXü*, which focuses on awakening deeper levels of consciousness so that we can return to *Xü* (the Void). Although the original meaning of *Xü* is cave, it is often translated into English as emptiness or void. In internal alchemy, (*Xü* refers to the highly refined spiritual state that allows us to understand the impermanence of everything, including money and fame, so that we are able to detach our hearts from the desires and suffering of the external world. *Xü* is also an advanced state in martial arts when the master makes her body feel so empty that her opponent is unable to find leverage against her.)

Martial Arts Principle: In the Dai Family XinYi system, one of the most important fighting rules is to move forward and not retreat. This means you will look for a way to move closer to the enemy the moment he moves to attack you. Mastering *ChangSanBu* will help you with this strategy. This martial arts principle is known as *JinFa* 進瀍—The Method of Moving Forward.

Chapter 5

WuXing QuanMu
五行拳母
The Mother Form of XinYi

變萬神 | 五行 | 散化

SanHua WuXing BianWanShen

Strew and transform the Five Elements to the Ten-Thousand-Spirits

HUANGTINGJING 黃庭經[1]

---

1   *HuangTingJing* 黃庭經 (The Yellow Court Classic) is a Daoist internal alchemy (*NeiDan* 內丹) text edited in 288 CE by Lady Wei HuaCun 魏華存, one of the most important founder masters of *ShangQing* 上清 (The Highest Purity School).

In the three remaining chapters, we will focus on methods that work with the fourth stage of our cultivation: *LiangXuHeDao* 煉虛合道 (Merging the Void with Dao)—three gives birth to Ten-Thousand-Things.

In this chapter, I will share *WuXing Quan* 五行拳, the Five Elements Form of the Dai Family XinYi system. According to the Daoist Five Elements philosophy, each Element has both Yin and Yang qualities and holds the features of all the Five Elements within. It is the interaction between and among the different elements that creates everything in existence—in other words, everything in the universe is created by the dynamics between the Five Elements. Following this fundamental Daoist principle, the XinYi Five Elements Form generates all other forms within the entire system. This is why the Five Elements Form is also called *MuQuan* 母拳, the Mother Form. As I mentioned earlier, I have chosen to focus the content of this book on actual XinYi practices, and I will not delve into the details of Five Elements philosophy and how it relates to the principle of Daoist internal alchemy.[2]

---

2   For those interested in learning more, my wife and I covered Five Elements philosophy and related internal alchemy principles in our book *Heavenly Stems and Earthly Branches—TianGan DiZhi: The Heart of Chinese Wisdom Traditions* (2014), also published by Singing Dragon.

5.1 *PiQuan* 劈拳
Metal Element Form

| 之 | 掇 | 捧 | 有 | 也 | 非 | 屬 | 似 | 劈 |
| 勢 | 碟 | 盤 | | | 斧 | 金 | 斧 | 拳 |

PiQuan SiFu ShuJin FeiFu Ye You PengPan ZhuoDie ZhiShi

PiQuan belongs to Metal and looks like an axe, but it is not an axe!
The momentum is of scooping up a precious platter

Movement: Starting from *WuJi Zhuang*, practice *LongShen* three times and then move your body into the *Su* posture of *ChangSanBu*, as described in section 4.2. We will use this as the opening sequence for each of the Five Elements Forms.

As you raise your hands along the central line of your body up toward your right cheek, curve your body into the *Su* position, curling your right hand into a fist. Your right forearm is twisted so that your right fist faces right. The flat of your left palm touches the back of your right fist.

As you straighten your body into the *Zhan* posture of *ChangSanBu*, twist your right forearm toward your center as you move your arms together up, forward, and then down as though you are drawing an arch. The flat of your left hand now touches the inside of your lower arm, with the tip of your left finger resting on the inner wrist crease of your right arm. End with both forearms horizontal in front of you, with elbows bent and close to your body.

Mirror this movement and practice alternating between your right and left sides.

Breath: Inhale as you curl into the *Su* posture and exhale as you extend into the *Zhan* posture.

Visualization: The momentum of this movement as you curl your body is somewhat scooping, as though you are moving to grab onto and lift a platter before raising your hands up to your cheek. As you extend your body, feel as though you are swinging an axe up, forward, and down before your arms come to rest in front of you.

*Figure 19: PiQuan Su
front view*

Figure 20: PiQuan Su side view

*Figure 21: PiQuan Zhan
front view*

Figure 22: PiQuan Zhan side view

Internal Alchemy Principle: The Chinese name for this form, *Pi* 劈, means chop, which suggests the movement itself mimics the downward chopping motion of a swinging axe. However, this chopping action is only half of the pattern. As we curl our bodies at the start of this movement, we also move slightly forward and up, as though getting ready to scoop up a large platter. It is easy to miss this subtle upward momentum that balances the strong downward thrust of the rest of the *PiQuan* movement.

PiQuan represents the Metal Element and is designed to strengthen your lung function. The spirit of lung, *BaiHu* 白虎 (White Tiger), uses powerful descending energy to break old patterns and inspire new ones. As we say in China, *ShenMingZaiYueHuXiJian* 生命在於呼吸間—Life is within the breath. From the traditional Chinese perspective, we mark our lives with our breath—beginning with the first breath at birth and ending with our last dying breath. Maintaining awareness of our breath throughout our lives helps encourage a healthy and powerful body. In internal alchemy cultivation, improving the function of our lung Qi is the first step toward spiritual transformation.

Martial Arts Principle: This is the first movement of the Five Elements and it helps to establish your martial power and cultivate your fearlessness in combat. When someone is attacking you, you can use this movement to bring him down, like *MengHuXiaShan* 猛虎下山—a formidable tiger running down the mountain. This movement emphasizes the downward or descending force of the Metal Element. However, please remember there is ascending force within the descending force. This martial arts principle is called *JiangFa* 降瀘—The Method of Descending.

5.2 *BengQuan* 崩拳
Wood Element Form

之｜浪｜舟｜有｜也｜非｜屬｜似｜崩
勢｜頭｜行｜　｜　｜箭｜木｜箭｜拳

BengQuan SiJian ShuMu FeiJian Ye You ZhouXing LangTou ZhiShi

BengQuan belongs to Wood and looks like an arrow, but it is not an arrow!
The momentum is of a sailboat rocking on the waves

Movement: From the opening sequence (starting from *WuJi Zhuang*, practice *LongShen* three times and then move your body into the *Su* posture of *ChangSanBu*, as described in section 4.2), curve your body as you make fists. Bringing them to rest on your right hip, the right fist faces heaven with the little finger side on the right hip, while the left fist faces earth with the thumb flush against the flat of your right fist.

Next, stretch your body and twist your arms in order to bring your fists in front of your chest. Turn your left fist to face your body and touch the midpoint of your chest, while moving your right fist forward and up until it reaches the same level as the tip of your nose.

Mirror this movement and then practice both sides alternately.

Breath: Inhale as you curve your body into the *Su* posture and exhale as you stretch into the *Zhan* posture.

Visualization: From the curled position, imagine your forward hand is like a stretched bow and your back hand is an arrow, armed and ready to fire. As you stretch your body, feel the bow-hand release as you bring it toward your chest whilst the arrow-hand shoots in front of your body. As you practice this movement, sense the rocking motion of your entire body as you curl and stretch, like a boat undulating on the water.

Figure 23: BengQuan Su front view

Figure 24: BengQuan Su side view

*Figure 25: BengQuan Zhan
front view*

Figure 26: BengQuan Zhan side view

Internal Alchemy Principle: *Beng* 崩 means stretched, tight, and release. The name of this form portrays the feeling of getting ready to shoot an arrow. The hidden feeling within this practice is the wave-like movement as you unfurl and elongate your whole body.

A Wood Element form, the *BengQuan* method provides a way to support the optimal function of your liver. In internal alchemy, the spirit of the liver is represented by *QingLong* 青龍 (Green Dragon), which has the energetic pattern of spiraling ascension. The Green Dragon spirit has the ability to break through and transform any obstacle.

Martial Arts Principle: If your opponent is much taller than you, this is a great movement to uproot him and shoot him away with your arrow-like fist, like *YunLongTanZhua* 雲龍探爪—cloudy dragon stretching his claw forward. Although this movement works with the ascending or uprising spiral force of the Wood Element, please remember there is downward force within it. This martial arts principle is called *ShengFa* 升灋—The Method of Ascending.

5.3 *ZuanQuan* 躦拳
Water Element Form

之	嶺	山	有	也	非	屬	似	躦
勢	塌	倒			閃	水	閃	拳

ZuanQuan SiShan ShuShui FeiShan Ye You ShanDao LingTa ZhiShi

ZuanQuan belongs to Water and looks like lightning, but is not lightning!
The momentum is that of landslide

Movement: From the opening sequence (from *WuJi Zhuang*, practice *LongShen* three times and then move your body into the *Su* posture of *ChangSanBu*, as described in section 4.2), raise your hands to the level of your chest, palms facing forward. Place your left hand on top of your right (with the fingers of the left hand touching the back of the right hand) as you curve your body. Make sure to bring your elbows in close to each other and close to your body.

Stretch your body and turn your hips so that your body faces left while twisting your right forearm so that your elbow points back toward your left foot and your right hand makes a loose fist. Bend your left arm so that your left hand rests on the center of your chest.

Now try mirroring this movement so that you can alternate the practice between your right and left sides.

Breath: Inhale as you curl into the *Su* posture and exhale as you stretch into the *Zhan* posture.

Visualization: Imagine your hands strike out like flashing lightning while you curve your body. When you stretch and turn into the next movement, feel as though your body is a landslide exploding from the peak of a great mountain.

*Figure 27: ZuanQuan Su
front view*

Figure 28: ZuanQuan Su side view

Figure 29: ZuanQuan front view

Figure 30: ZuanQuan side view

Internal Alchemy Principle: *Zuan* 躦 means jump up and dash forward. The movement is light and quick like lightning. On the other hand, the movement also embodies the heaviness of boulders and mountains.

As a Water Element form, *ZuanQuan* is a way to cultivate your kidney energy. In internal alchemy, the spirit of the kidney is *XuanWu* 玄武, the Mystical Warrior (turtle and snake), which moves in surges as water does. The hidden power of the Mystical Warrior spirit nourishes the roots of your life energy and helps awaken your inner wisdom.

Martial Arts Principle: During an attack, you can move quickly to receive the force from your opponent with your hands or forearms, like *BaiSheTuXin* 白蛇吐信—the white snake strikes out its forked tongue, and then immediately retract the force by turning your hips and besting your opponent with your shoulder, like *LingGuiZhuanShen* 靈龜轉身—the spiritual turtle turns its body. While this movement works with the holding or locking force of the Water Element, please remember the opening and releasing force within it. This martial arts principle is known as *HeFa* 合瀘— The Method of Uniting.

5.4 *PaoQuan* 炮拳
Fire Element Form

之	排	江	有	也	非	屬	似	炮
勢	岸	水			砲	火	砲	拳

PaoQuan SiPao ShuHuo FeiPao Ye You JiangShui PaiAn ZhiShi

PaoQuan belongs to Fire and looks like a cannon ball,
but is not a cannon ball!
The momentum is the rippling effect of water

Movement: From the opening sequence (from *WuJi Zhuang*, practice *LongShen* three times before moving your body into the *Su* posture of *ChangSanBu*, as described in section 4.2), raise your hands to the level of your mouth and cross your wrists with the left wrist on top of the right. Both palms are relaxed and fingers point downward as you curve your body, with elbows dropped and held close to each other and close to your body.

Stretching your body, circle your wrists forward (from your body) as you make fists. With the left hand still on top of your right, pound your (upward facing) fists downward until your forearms are parallel with the earth. Your elbows are still held close to each other and to your body.

Practice this movement, alternating between the left and right sides.

Breath: Inhale as you move into curving your body, and exhale as you move into stretching your body.

Visualization: As you curve your body, imagine that within your arms and chest you hold a cannon ball that is just about to explode outwards. When you move into the stretch and make your fists, feel your body as powerful as a ring of waves expanding outwards in all directions.

Figure 31: PaoQuan Su
front view

Figure 32: PaoQuan Su side view

Figure 33: PaoQuan Zhan front view

Figure 34: PaoQuan Zhan side view

Internal Alchemy Principle: The original meaning of *Pao* 炮 is a special type of roasting style in which we pack game in mud and place it directly in the fire to roast. Once it is ready, the dried mud casing cracks with a powerful noise of explosion. It is also commonly used to mean cannon or cannon ball.

When you practice this movement, you will experience both the sense of explosion as well as an expansive wave-like feeling. *PaoQuan* is a Fire Element practice and is a way to strengthen your heart function and to balance your Yin and Yang energies. In internal alchemy, the spirit of the heart is *ZhuQue* 朱雀 (Red Bird), which moves upwards like a flame. The spirit of the Red Bird brings the element of joy into both your practice and your daily life and enriches your experience of your own spirituality.

Martial Arts Principle: If your opponent either comes in to attack the central line of your body or tries to use two hands to attack you on both sides, you can apply this movement to defeat him, like *HeChongJiuTian* 鶴沖九天—crane soars into the ninth heaven.[3] This movement uses the opening and upward force of the Fire Element, yet there is also fastening and downward force within it. This martial arts principle is known as *KaiFa* 開灋—The Method of Exposing.

---

3   According to Chinese mythology, there are nine heavens; the ninth heaven is the highest heaven.

5.5 *HengQuan* 橫拳
Earth Element Form

橫拳　似彈　屬土　非彈　也　有　輪行　豪溝　之勢

HengQuan SiDan ShuTu FeiDan Ye You LunXing HaoGou ZhiShi

HengQuan belongs to Earth and looks like a
rolling ball, but is not a rolling ball!
The momentum is of a wheel moving out of a deep rut

Movement: From the opening sequence (starting from *WuJi Zhuang*, practice *LongShen* three times and then move your body into the *Su* posture of *ChangSanBu*, as described in section 4.2), curve your body and make a fist with your right hand, turning it up, with the fist facing heaven. At the same time, keep your left palm open, facing earth, and in contact with your right fist. Bring both arms down so that your elbows touch your lower belly.

As you stretch your body, turn both hands together 90 degrees to the left as you move them upward and forward to the level of your chest. Keep your elbows in contact with your body.

Switch sides and practice this movement, alternating left and right.

Breath: Inhale as you move into curving your body, and exhale as you move into stretching your body.

Visualization: The sensation as you curve your body is like a rolling ball trundling down to your *DanTian*. Once you stretch your body, the upward momentum is like a wheel finally freeing itself from a deep rut.

Figure 35: HengQuan Su front view

Figure 36: HengQuan Su side view

Figure 37: HengQuan Zhan front view

Figure 38: HengQuan Zhan side view

Internal Alchemy Principle: *Heng* 橫 means the bar latch of an old-style door, side, east to west, horizontal, transverse, broad, cover, interlock, bossy, and tough. When you practice this movement, you will have the sense of swinging back and forth or riding your bike over a series of speed bumps.

As an Earth Element practice, this form boosts your spleen Qi and digestive function to improve your ability to nourish all parts of your body. In internal alchemy, the spirit of the spleen is *HuangPo* 黃婆 (Yellow Lady). The Yellow Lady is the central coordinator, much like the axis of a wheel. This movement helps you to develop great stability and the ability to harmonize your life.

Martial Arts Principle: You may utilize this movement during any kind of attack, like *FengHuangDianTou* 鳳凰點頭—phoenix nods her head. This movement makes use of the swinging and horizontal forces of the Earth Element while at the same time incorporating a snapping and vertical force within. This martial arts principle is known as *HeFa* 和瀮—The Method of Harmonizing.

Chapter 6

LiuHe XinYi 六合心意

Advanced Approach

放彌六合 ｜ 卷藏心意

FangMiLiuHe JuanChangXinYi

Expanding to fill up the Universe
Coiling to store within the Heart-Mind

XINYI PROVERB
(PASSED THROUGH ORAL TRADITION)

The name of a traditional martial arts or Qigong school offers insight into the spirit of its system. To deepen your understanding of the XinYi system and help you to grow into a high-level practitioner, I will now explore the meaning behind the name of the XinYi system with you.

6.1 *XinYi LiuHe* 心意六合 The Universe within Me

Although the original full name for the Dai Family XinYi martial arts system is *XinYi LiuHe Quan* 心意六合拳, it is also called *LiuHe XinYi Quan* 六合心意拳, *LiuHe Quan* 六合拳, or *XinYi Quan* 心意拳. The latter is the one now commonly used. It was martial artists outside of the Dai Family who later added "Dai Family" to the title.

Literally, *Xin* means heart and *Yi* means mind. As the name XinYi implies, we need to use both our heart and our mind to learn and practice this system—and vice versa, practicing with this martial arts tradition is also a way to cultivate your heart and mind. In both respects, XinYi is not a system that focuses solely on the mastery of physical fighting skills.

Liu means six and *He* means combine, combination, cooperate, unite, and union. *LiuHe* means "the Union of Six" and it is a Daoist philosophical phrase used interchangeably with "universe." The Chinese expression for universe is *YuZhou* 宇宙[1]—the union of space and time. As I mentioned in section 4.1 during my discussion about the Trinity, in Daoist philosophy each individual object or concept consists of three parts. With respect to the universe, *Yu* contains the *Shang* 上 (upper), *Zhong* 中 (middle), and *Xia* 下 (lower) components of space and, within *Zhou*, the *Gu* 古 (ancient or past), *Jin* 今 (modern or present), and *Lai* 來 (future or upcoming) create the inseparable aspects of time. The universe itself is the union of these six factors, and the true meaning of *LiuHe* is the union of the three dimensions of space and the three dimensions of time. *XinYi LiuHe Quan*, the Dai family internal alchemy and martial arts system, was intentionally and mindfully created to help the practitioner emulate with the Universal Way.

---

1   *Yu* 宇 means space and *Zhou* 宙 means time.

Quan 拳 means fist, and is generally used to represent a form or a system of martial arts. However, in the inner teachings of the XinYi internal martial arts system, we learn the true meaning of *Quan* is not *Quan* 拳, but *Quan* 圈, which means circle or circular. In the XinYi system, we always practice with circular movements and use the circle—not the fist—to defeat our opponents. There is not a single movement in the entire system that does not include round patterns. *XinYi Quan* is a method of internal cultivation that aligns the practitioner with the circle—the Way of Heaven.

The *XinYi LiuHe Quan* Heart-Mind cultivation methods provide a key to the Oneness state, a palpable feeling of no separation between human being and the Dao where there is no difference between man and nature. In China, we describe this as *YuZhouZaiWuShen WuShenZaiYuZhou* 宇宙在吾身吾身在宇宙—The universe is within me and I am the universe. To awaken into this high-level martial arts state during combat training we must know how to unite the three dimensions of time and the three dimensions of space in our body and in all of our movements.

In the XinYi system there are many layers of *LiuHe* that guide our training. For instance, one of the most important meanings of *LiuHe* is described as being made of two parts: the internal three unions and external three unions. The internal three unions are:

氣　意　心
與　與　與
力　氣　意
合　合　合

XinYuYiHe YiYuQiHe QiYuLiHe

Heart unites with mind
Mind unites with Qi
Qi unites with force

The internal three unions help us to instill the concept of Oneness in time (past, present, and future) into our movement, especially during real combat.

The external three unions are:

手 肘 肩
與 與 與
足 膝 跨
合 合 合

JianYuKuaHe ZhouYuXiHe ShouYuZuHe

Shoulders unite with hips
Elbows unite with knees
Hands unite with feet

Training with the three external unions helps us to master the Oneness of space (upper, middle, and lower) in our movements as well as making our use of space come alive in times of combat, when timing is crucial.

In the first stage of training we focus on the *LiuHe* of the six spiritual animals (see section 2.2.2). However, in the highest level of training, we follow this guidance about *LiuHe*:

勁 神 心 體 靜 動
與 與 與 與 與 與
虛 勁 神 心 體 靜
合 合 合 合 合 合

DongYuJingHe JingYuTiHe TiYuXinHe XinYuShenHe ShenYuJingHe JingYuXüHe

The movement unites with tranquility
Tranquility unites with the body
The body unites with the heart
The heart unites with spirit
The spirit unites with power
Power unites with emptiness

In the following section, I will introduce one of the XinYi methods used to cultivate *LiuHe* within your body.

6.2 *LiuHe XinFa* 六合心瀍
The Six Unions Heart Method

This advanced practice is based on the special Dai Family *LiuHe Zhuang* 六合椿—Six Unions Stance, which works with the internal three unions and external three unions. These practices help the practitioner master the union of time and space, and feel the state of Oneness of the universe.

Movement: Starting from the opening sequence (from *WuJi Zhuang*, practice *LongShen* three times and then curve your body into the *Su* posture of *ChangSanBu*), turn your hip and upper body to the right and keep your head upright and facing forward. At the same time, raise your right palm to touch the left side of your chest and lower your left hand to stretch between your thighs with fingers pointing toward earth. The left arm is twisted so that your left palm faces left and your left shoulder is pointing forward.

Maintain this posture for at least 5–10 minutes before trying the same movement on the opposite side, holding it for at least another 5–10 minutes.

After you have practiced this *LiuHe* posture correctly for approximately three continuous months, gradually speed up the rhythm of switching between the right and left sides. Once you are comfortable with this, you can add a step each time you switch and begin the special stepping method called *LiuHeBu* 六合步. Advanced practitioners practice the *LiuHeBu* in a ceremonial *QiXing* 七星 (Big Dipper) pattern. As you progress, I hope you will be able to find a qualified teacher to share these advanced practices with you. The finer details required to keep moving you to the highest levels of this practice must be taught on a one-on-one basis.

Breath: Adjust your breathing to be slow, smooth, deep, and even. Breathe with your lungs, with your skin, and with your navel. Imagine all the pores of your skin open to allow the universal Qi, like sunlight, to surround you and enter into your body. Gather all of this Qi into your navel with each inhalation. With each exhalation, feel the Qi descend from your navel into your *DanTian*.

Figure 39: Right LiuHe Zhuang front view

Figure 40: Right LiuHe Zhuang side view

*Figure 41: Left LiuHe
Zhuang front view*

Figure 42: Left LiuHe Zhuang side view

Visualization: Imagine that your whole body is growing transparent and merging into a Qi field of universal Qi. Feel that you are no longer separate from the universe—you are within the universe, and the universe is within you.

Internal Alchemy Principle: In the last stage of internal alchemy practice, we work with *Xü* (Emptiness) in order to live with the reality of the Dao. This is called *LiangXüHeDao* 煉虛合道—Merging the Void with the Dao. Although *Xü* has come to mean emptiness, hollow, and void, the original meaning of *Xü* was a cave—the original dwelling place of our early ancestral human beings. The cave is the symbol for the place where the Dao and heart reside, and it also symbolizes the prenatal state. *LiuHe XinFa* is a way to guard your heart-cave and cultivate *Xü*.

Martial Arts Principle: In martial arts, *Xü* describes the state of *XingYuLiuShui* 行雲流水, where the practitioner's physical movement and internal Qi are as smooth as freely moving clouds and flowing water. Waiting until the moment your attacker almost touches you, use *LiuHeBu* to quickly shift your body, avoid his force, and make your own attack. This martial arts principle is known as *KongFa* 空灋—The Method of Emptiness.

Chapter 7

BaGua XinJing 八卦心鏡
Achieve Enlightenment

象在其中｜八卦成列

BaGuaChengLie XiangZaiQiZhong

Eight trigrams create the arrangement
All images are within

YIJING, XICI 系辭

(APPENDED STATEMENTS)

In this chapter, we will continue our focus on XinYi methods that work with 煉虛合道 (Merging the Void with the Dao), the final stage of our cultivation practice through which we are able to reach the highest level of martial arts training. It is in these methods that we pursue *WuXing* 無形—the formless. Formless does not simply mean without form; rather, its true meaning is when a master fully grasps the spirit of forms she has been practicing and is able to merge them into her simple daily activities. We may not be able to tell the master is practicing martial arts because it appears as though she is casually walking or doing ordinary daily work. Similarly, it may be difficult for us to distinguish which martial arts movement the master has utilized the moment she defeats her competitor. Within the XinYi system there is a common saying to describe such formlessness:

不　倘　不　拳
為　若　見　打
能　見　形　三
　　形　　　節

QuanDaSanJie BuXianXing TangRouXianXing BuWeiNeng

Defeat others with the Trinity
Do not show your technique
If you reveal your technique
You are not talented!

The state of formlessness results from mastering the three levels—physical body, high consciousness, and inner wisdom—of any martial arts system. In the Dai Family XinYi system, once we have completed the training discussed in Chapters 2–6 we can move on to practice *BaGua XinJing* 八卦心鏡, which helps us work with formlessness.

The *BaGua XinJing* are eight *YinRou* 陰柔 (soft, gentle movements) that are associated with the *BaGua* of the *YiJing*. *BaGua* 八卦 means Eight Trigrams. In the *YiJing* there are two trigram arrangements: *XianTian BaGua* 先天八卦 (Prenatal Trigrams Arrangement) and *HouTian BaGua* 後天八卦 (Postnatal Trigrams Arrangement).[1] According to the Daoist *YiJing* divination system,

---

1   The diagrams of the two *BaGua* arrangements (Figures 43 and 44) are cited from my book *Seeking the Spirit of The Book of Change* (2009), also published by Singing Dragon. If interested, you will find details about the symbolic and numerological meanings of the *BaGua* there.

these two BaGua arrangements create a mirror of the universe that reflects all things. In this chapter, I will include some principles of the pre- and postnatal arrangements as they relate to XinYi practice.

XinJing 心鏡 means heart-mirror. In Chinese wisdom traditions, the mirror represents the heart itself, as it is through our hearts that we are able to see most clearly. In ancient China, mirrors were made from bronze and, in order to maintain a reflective surface, they had to be polished on a regular basis. When we cannot see things clearly it is because our hearts are buried under *HongChen* 紅塵, Red Dust,[2] much like tarnished or corroded bronze. The *XinJing* is an essential *MingJing* 明鏡[3] method to keep our heart-mirror bright and clean, to help us to act from our hearts during our martial arts practice, and to support us on our path to Enlightenment. In fact, another name for the XinYi martial arts system is *ShouDongChenJi* 守洞塵技,[4] which describes the practice as an art of protecting our personal territory in the world of "dust"—one that protects us from harm both physically and spiritually.

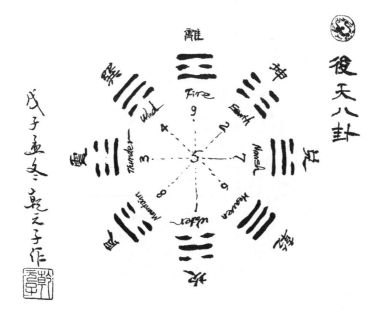

Figure 43: HouTian BaGua 後天八卦—*Postnatal Trigrams Arrangement*

---

2 In Chinese wisdom traditions, Red Dust refers to any object or event that tempts us into filling our hearts with desire, anger, ignorance, pride, or jealousy, causing us to lose our sense of our own true nature.

3 *Ming* 明 (bright, brightness), *Jing* 鏡 (mirror) = "Bright Mirror."

4 *Shou* 守 (maintain, protect, hold, defend, guard), *Dong* 洞 (cave), *Chen* 塵 (dust), *Ji* 技 (art, technique).

Figure 44: XianTian BaGua 先天八卦—*Prenatal Trigrams Arrangement*

*Figure 45: Tang Dynasty bronze mirror with the HouTian BaGua Arrangement,
encircling the Mystical Warrior (excavated in Xi'An, ShaanXi Province in 1971)*

The eight movements of *BaGua XinJing* are commonly known as *MoJingMoJing* 磨鏡抹勁. *Mo* 磨 means grind and polish; *Jing* 鏡 means mirror, clarity, and to see yourself clearly;[5] *Mo* 抹 means touch, searching, cleaning, and mopping; *Jing* 勁 means inner force or power. Together, *MoJingMoJing* means polishing your mirror to increase your power.

Through regular practice of these eight slow movements, you will be able to progressively awaken your consciousness and come to understand the heart of all martial arts. Grandmaster Zhao often tells his students that in order to become a skillful XinYi practitioner we must have the intelligence to understand the system and the dedication to practice with our physical body, our mind, and our heart.

---

5 As mentioned, the mirror represents the heart, and a clear mirror symbolizes a pure heart, full of wisdom.

7.1 ☰ *Qian* 乾
Heaven

Movement: Starting from *WuJi Zhuang*, practice *LongShen* three times and then step to the right to come into *MaBu Zhuang* 馬步椿 (horse stance), with your upper body curved in the *Su* posture, as described in section 3.2, and keeping your hands touching your lower belly. This is the opening sequence to each movement of the *BaGua XinJing*.

Keeping your right leg slightly bent, straighten your left leg and shift your upper body to the right, while keeping your head upright and facing straight ahead. At the same time, while keeping contact with your body, draw an arch from your lower belly over the left ribcage to your right upper chest with your right hand. If you are familiar with acupuncture points, continue the arch until your right *LaoGong* 勞宫 covers your right *QiHu* 氣戶 ("Gate of Qi," also known as ST13) point. Your left hand also maintains direct contact with your body, arching slightly to the lower left of your torso.

Try the same movement on the reverse side: Gradually shift your upper body back to the center to return to *MaBu Zhuang*. Keeping your left leg slightly bent, straighten your right leg and shift your upper body to the left. At the same time, while keeping contact with your body, draw an arch from your lower belly over the right ribcage to your left upper chest with your left hand. Your right hand also maintains direct contact with your body, arching slightly to the lower right of your torso.

Practice the above movements, alternating smoothly between the right and left sides, for at least 5–10 minutes. Make sure to harmonize the four spiritual gates during your movements—coordinating the movement of your right hip to right shoulder as you move right, and left hip to left shoulder as you move left.

Breath: Inhale as your body shifts toward the center and exhale as your body moves away from the center.

Visualization: Imagine there is a golden ball of light spinning in your lower belly as you practice this movement. Feel the entire universe is within your body.

Figure 46: Qian—
stretching right

Figure 47: Qian—stretching left

Internal Alchemy Principle: This movement models the trigram ☰ *Qian* (Heaven). The three unbroken Yang lines in this trigram represent the Heavenly Way, unbroken and continuous, the strength of the universe, the power of nature, circular, and round shape—much like gazing far into the heavens brings us a sense of roundness and eternity. Keeping this endless circle within your body during your practice opens up the energy gates within your whole body and allows the Qi to circulate freely. In just a few minutes of this practice, you will start to generate a lot of internal heat. The *Qian* practice particularly works to open the four spiritual gates of the body (the major joints—the shoulders, hips), which are the root of the *LiuHe* (Six Unions),[6] and helps strengthen the bones and regulate the function of the large intestines. Through this practice, we deepen our understanding of space and time within the body and unite the physical and spiritual body into one.

In the south or top position of the postnatal and prenatal BaGua arrangements, we find the trigrams ☲ *Li*/ Fire and ☰ *Qian*/ Heaven, respectively.[7] The combination of these two trigrams creates the hexagram ䷍ *DaYou* 大有 (Great Provider or Enricher). According to *BaGua* symbolism, the trigram *Li*/Fire represents the heart (*Xin*) and the trigram *Qian*/Heaven represents a mirror (*Jing*). While *DaYou* symbolizes the first movement in the *XinJing* sequence, it also encapsulates the principle of the entire XinYi method. This system teaches us that true power is born in the heart. Polishing your heart, the Great Mirror and Great Provider, brings richness into your martial arts and spiritual cultivation practice.

Martial Arts Principle: In martial arts, your territory is the space taken up by your body at any given time. One of the most essential principles of XinYi combat is to hold your space, much like a tiger protects its den. This movement teaches us to maintain our center by keeping our arms and hands close to our body, how to master our sense of space by coordinating the Six Unions, and how to access the inner power generated by a purified heart. The martial arts principle associated with the movement is called *YuanTongFa* 圓通灋—The Method of Circulating and Flowing.

---

6   From section 6.1. The internal Six Unions are: Heart-Mind, Mind-Qi, and Qi-Force. The external Six Unions are: shoulders–hips, elbows–knees, and wrists–ankles.

7   In the traditional Chinese mapping system, south is always located on the top, with north at the bottom, east on the left, and west on the right. Both *BaGua* arrangements follow this tradition.

7.2 ☱ *Dui* 兌
Marsh/Lake

Movement: From the starting sequence (from *WuJi Zhuang*, practice *LongShen* three times before stepping to the right into *MaBu Zhuang* with your upper body in the *Su* posture), keep your right leg slightly bent, straighten your left leg, and shift your upper body to the right. Your head is upright and facing forward. At the same time, make loose fists with both hands. With your right fist facing your body, make an arch with your right fist from the left side of your lower belly through the left ribcage, past your chin, and to your right cheek. As you move, slowly roll your right fist so that you end with your right fist facing away from your body. Keep your right fist and elbow close to your body through the entire movement.

Slowly shift your body back to *MaBu Zhuang*. Next, try the same move for the left side. Keeping your left leg slightly bent, straighten your right leg and shift your upper body to the left. At the same time, move your right fist down to your lower belly and arch your left fist from the right side of your lower belly through the right ribcage, past your chin, and to your left cheek. As you move, slowly roll your left fist so that you end with your left fist facing away from your body. Keep your left fist and elbow close to your body through the entire movement.

Please practice the movement, alternating right and left for at least 5–10 minutes.

Breath: Inhale as you contract toward the center and exhale as you expand away from the center. Connect with the YinYang energy within your body through each breath.

Visualization: As you move right and left, imagine you are opening the floodgates, allowing the Qi to flow and creating space for opportunities to arise.

*Figure 48: Dui—
stretching right*

Figure 49: Dui—stretching left

Internal Alchemy Principle: This movement models the trigram ☱ *Dui* (Marsh or Lake). The pattern of trigram *Dui* is made of two solid Yang lines below one broken Yin line, and represents openness, mouth, marsh, lake, communication, exchange, trade, break, and more. We need to be able to break some of our old patterns if we are truly committed to evolving into new ways of being through our internal cultivation. This practice helps us to move through stagnant patterns, work through physical and mental weaknesses and rebuild healthy ways of living, and helps optimize the function of the lungs.

From the southeast direction (or top-left position) of the *BaGua* diagrams, we can see the trigrams *Xun*/Wind and *Dui*/Marsh. From the joining of these two trigrams, the hexagram ䷼ *ZhongFu* 中孚—Inner Faith/Trust is born. *ZhongFu* works to build confidence in your martial power and come to trust the inherent self-healing mechanisms within your body.

Martial Arts Principle: This movement helps break the typical external martial arts blocking and attacking techniques. If someone comes toward you as if to attack, this movement teaches you how to shift your body so that the oncoming force from your opponent is used against him and leaves you in control of the situation. This martial arts principle is known as *QiHuaFa* 炁化灋—The Method of Qi/Energy Transforming.

7.3 ☲ *Li* 離
Fire

Movement: From the starting sequence (from *WuJi Zhuang*, practice *LongShen* three times before stepping to the right into *MaBu Zhuang* with your upper body in the *Su* posture), raise your hands to your chest level with palms facing each other, as though you are holding a ball of Qi.

Keeping your right leg slightly bent, straighten your left leg and shift your upper body to the right. Keep your head upright and facing forward. At the same time, rotate the ball of Qi so that your right palm is at the level of your right shoulder and facing earth while your left palm is at the level of your lower *DanTian* and facing heaven. Feel the connection between your *LaoGong*.

Next, try the same movement on the left side: Slowly shift back into *MaBu Zhuang* and continue moving your upper body toward the left by keeping your left leg slightly bent and straightening your right leg. Keep your head upright and facing forward. At the same time, rotate the ball of Qi so that your left palm is at the level of your left shoulder and facing earth while your right palm is at the level of your lower *DanTian* and facing heaven. Feel the connection between your *LaoGong*.

Please practice the movements, alternating left and right, for at least 5–10 minutes.

Figure 50: Li—center

Figure 51: Li—stretching right

Figure 52: Li—stretching left

Breath: Inhale as you contract toward the center and exhale as you expand away from the center.

Visualization: Imagine your hands holding the sun, rotating between your hands, as you move from side to side. Do not drop it!

Internal Alchemy Principle: This movement represents the trigram ☲ *Li* (Fire). The trigram *Li* is made up of two solid Yang lines at the top and bottom with one broken Yin line in the center. *Li* represents the heart, brightness, joy, colorful, armor, and anything armored. Notice that your hand positions mirror the structure of the trigram itself, outer hard and inner soft—this practice is the image of the protector. With this movement we are also strengthening the function of the heart and our external Qi.

In the eastern-direction (left) positions of the *BaGua* diagrams, we can see the trigram *Zhen*/Thunder (postnatal) and *Li*/Fire (prenatal). Together, these trigrams make the ䷶ *Feng* 豐 (Harvest) hexagram. This is a practice of great Qi harvest, leading to increased health, happiness, and longevity.

Martial Arts Principle: This movement works with *Gun* 滾, the rolling force. During an attack you can use this movement to roll your opponent's force away from him and then gently back to overthrow him. This martial arts principle is *XuGunFa* 虛滾灋—The Method of Voiding and Rolling.

7.4 ☳ *Zhen* 震
Thunder

Movement: From the starting sequence (from *WuJi Zhuang*, practice *LongShen* three times before stepping to the right into *MaBu Zhuang* with your upper body in the *Su* posture), raise your hands up the central line, with palms facing heaven. When you reach the level of your chest, turn your right hand so that your palm faces forward and bring your left palm down to the level of your *DanTian*.

As you straighten your right leg, turn your hips and upper body about 45 degrees to the left and push your right palm forward, arching 45 degrees toward the left. At the same time, move your left elbow straight behind you so that your left palm comes to the level of your left hip. Keep your head upright and facing forward.

Gradually shift your body back into *MaBu Zhuang*. Next try the movement on the left side. Raise your left hand to the level of your middle *DanTian* as you turn your left palm to face forward while moving your right palm down to your lower *DanTian* with palm facing heaven.

As you straighten your left leg, turn your hips and upper body about 45 degrees to the right and push your left palm forward, arching 45 degrees toward the right. At the same time, move your right elbow straight behind you so that your right palm, facing heaven, comes to the level of your right hip. Keep your head upright and facing forward.

Please alternate the movements on both the right and left sides for 5–10 minutes.

Breath: Inhale as you contract toward the center and exhale as you expand away from the center.

Visualization: Imagine your arms as flying dragons shuttling in and out of the clouds.

*Figure 53: Zhen—
right center*

Figure 54: Zhen—stretching right

Figure 55: Zhen—left center

Figure 56: Zhen—stretching left

Internal Alchemy Principle: This movement models the trigram ☳ *Zhen* (Thunder), which is one Yang line below two Yin lines. Some of the symbolic meanings of *Zhen* include shaking, thunder, move, unstable, vibrate, and Yang energy pushing out like the sprouts of the early spring breaking through the earth. The movement helps to boost the immune system, improve gallbladder function, create Yang Qi, and uplift your spirits.

In the northeast direction (left-lower position) of the *BaGua* diagrams, we find the trigrams *Gen*/Mountain and *Zhen*/Thunder. The combination of these two trigrams makes the hexagram ䷚ *Yi* 頤—Nourish. This practice stimulates your Yang Qi and helps awaken your *ZhengQi* 正炁, the righteous Qi within our bodies, which is then used to nourish all aspects of your life.

Martial Arts Principle: This movement teaches you the unseating power of the thrusting force. During an attack you can use this movement to deflect oncoming forces and strike back, all in the same moment. It is especially helpful if your opponent is someone who is physically much stronger than you are. The diagonal movement between the shoulders and hips is key here—this is how you will be able to easily shake off someone who is twice your size! The martial arts principle of this movement is *XiangLongFa* 降龍瀍—The Method of Subduing the Dragon.

7.5 ☴ *Xun* 巽
Wind

Movement: From the starting sequence (from *WuJi Zhuang*, practice *LongShen* three times before stepping to the right into *MaBu Zhuang* with your upper body in the *Su* posture), raise your right hand to your right armpit with palm facing slightly left and upward while you turn your left palm facing earth and bring it close to your left hip.

Straighten your right leg as you shift your upper body toward the left and slowly rotate your right forearm and move it forward with right palm facing heaven and thrusting the right fingers in front of you. Bring your left elbow further back, keeping your left palm facing earth and in line with your left hip. Throughout this movement, keep your head upright and facing forward.

Gradually move back into *MaBu Zhuang* and practice the same movement on the left side. Raise your left hand to your left armpit with palm facing slightly right and upward while you turn your right palm facing earth and bring it close to your right hip.

Straighten your left leg as you shift your upper body toward the right and slowly rotate your left forearm and move it forward with left palm facing heaven and thrusting the left fingers in front of you. Bring your right elbow further back, keeping your right palm facing earth and in line with your right hip. Throughout this movement, keep your head upright and facing forward.

Please practice alternating this movement right and left for at least 5–10 minutes.

Breath: Inhale as you contract toward the center and exhale as you expand away from the center.

Visualization: Imagine your fingers as arrows shooting forward when your hand moves in front of your body, and feel your back hand as a metal rake grating backward as you move toward your hip.

Figure 57: Xun—right center

Figure 58: Xun—stretching right

Figure 59: Xun—left center

Figure 60: Xun—stretching left

Internal Alchemy Principle: This is the movement of the trigram ☴ *Xun* (Wind). *Xun* is made of one Yin line below two Yang lines. It is the symbol for the power of the wind, which can be subtle and hidden, yet incredibly strong and potentially destructive. The movement helps increase life energy, improve liver and digestion function, and transform feelings of depression.

The southwest direction (or right-upper position) of the *BaGua* diagrams is where we find the trigrams *Kun*/Earth and *Xun*/Wind. The combination of these trigrams makes the hexagram ䷭ *Shen* 升—Arise. This practice helps to build confidence, uplift your Qi, and raise your skill level in battle.

Martial Arts Principle: This movement demonstrates the powerful spiraling force of Yin and Yang. During an attack, you can use this movement to draw in your opponent's force or to totally blow them away. This martial arts principle is called *XuanFengFa* 旋風濾—The Method of Spinning Wind.

7.6 ☵ *Kan* 坎
Water

Movement: From the starting sequence (from *WuJi Zhuang*, practice *LongShen* three times before stepping to the right into *MaBu Zhuang* with your upper body in the *Su* posture), raise your hands to your chest level with right palm facing heaven and left palm facing earth. Your forearms are parallel to each other.

Keeping your arms and shoulders stable and turning from your hips, bring your upper body and arms toward your right side, continuing as far as you can. Throughout the movement, keep your head and upper body upright.

Gradually move back to *MaBu Zhuang*, turning your palms over so that your right palm is now facing earth and the left palm faces heaven. As before, turn your arms and body, this time toward the left, continuing as far as you can. Remember to turn from the hips while keeping your head and upper body upright.

Please practice these movements, alternating between right and left sides, for at least 5–10 minutes.

Breath: Inhale as you contract toward the center and exhale as you expand away from the center.

Visualization: Imagine yourself in the center of a Qi vortex as you turn your body left and right.

Figure 61: Kan—
right center

Figure 62: Kan—turning right

Figure 63: Kan—
turning far right

Figure 64: Kan—left center

*Figure 65: Kan—
turning left*

Figure 66: Kan—turning far left

Internal Alchemy Principle: This is the movement of the trigram ☵ *Kan* (Water). *Kan* is one Yang line nested within two Yin lines. It symbolizes hidden power, danger, trap, uneven, skill, and wisdom. The vicissitudes of life are like a series of waves. During our cultivation practice, we learn not to become trapped by any difficulties that arise in our lives but instead to ride the waves with grace, moving around or transforming obstacles as we can. The movement helps strengthen our *Jing* 精, the very essence of our lives, enhances the function of our kidneys, and nourishes our *Shen* 神—which includes both our spirit and brain.

In the western direction or right position of the *BaGua* diagrams, we see the trigrams *Dui*/Marsh and *Kan*/Water. Together, these two trigrams make the hexagram ䷜ *Kun* 困—Bundle. The practice helps us work through any difficult situations that may leave us feeling trapped and powerless and helps awaken our inner wisdom.

Martial Arts Principle: This movement demonstrates the power of the inner wave and the force of Yang within the *DanTian*. If someone is attempting to grab, punch, or push you, this movement will help you slip easily through his grasp. Please remember that the moment it appears as though all hope is lost, you may be able to find a golden window of opportunity and, conversely, the moment you take for granted that all is safe, the tide could turn, tumbling you toward disaster. This martial arts principle is called *BoLangFa* 波浪瀘— The Method of Waves and Tides.

7.7 ☶ Gen 艮
Mountain

Movement: From the starting sequence (from *WuJi Zhuang*, practice *LongShen* three times before stepping to the right into *MaBu Zhuang* with your upper body in the *Su* posture), straighten your left leg and shift your upper body to the right. At the same time, turn your left palm to face earth and stretch your left arm down your left side as you turn your right palm to face heaven, drawing an arch to the front of your right shoulder as you stretch toward the right. Keep your right elbow tucked in close to the right ribcage, your head upright, and face forward.

Slowly shift back into *MaBu Zhuang*. Straighten your right leg and shift your upper body to the left. At the same time, turn your right palm to face earth and stretch your right arm down your right side as you turn your left palm to face heaven, drawing an arch to the front of your left shoulder as you stretch toward the left. Keep your left elbow tucked in close to the left ribcage, your head upright, and face forward.

Please practice this movement, alternating between the right and left sides, for at least 5–10 minutes.

Breath: Inhale as you contract toward the center and exhale as you expand away from the center.

Visualization: Imagine you are riding the yellow phoenix through the peaks and valleys of the mountains as you move your body from side to side.

Figure 67: Gen—
stretching right

Figure 68: Gen—stretching left

Internal Alchemy Principle: This movement mirrors the trigram ☶ *Gen* (Mountain). *Gen* is made of two Yin lines below one Yang line and symbolizes a mountain, stability, rooted, mature, everlasting, and more. It is fundamentally important to stay grounded, emotionally steady, and physically stable in our martial arts and internal alchemy practice and in our daily lives. This practice helps you to physically anchor into your root, strengthen your spleen Qi and digestive function, and stay mentally and emotionally focused.

In the northwestern direction or bottom-right position of the *BaGua* diagrams, we find the trigrams *Qian*/Heaven and *Gen*/Mountain. These two trigrams produce the hexagram ䷠ *Dun* 遯—Retreat. Daily practice of this movement helps you learn to draw your energy and spirit back into the center of your body.

Martial Arts Principle: This movement helps to develop your skills in utilizing your joints in combat. Use the joints on one side of your body to contact your opponent while using the joints on the other side of your body to throw him off balance. This martial arts principle is known as *FuHuFa* 伏虎瀍—The Method of Conquering the Tiger.

7.8 ☷ *Kun* 坤
Earth

Movement: From the starting sequence (from *WuJi Zhuang*, practice *LongShen* three times before stepping to the right into *MaBu Zhuang* with your upper body in the *Su* posture), make loose fists and raise your right fist to face your right cheek. Keep your right elbow down and tucked in close to your body as you bring your left fist under your right elbow. Next, straighten your right leg and turn your upper body toward the left as you twist your right forearm to bring your right fist close to your left cheek. As before, keep your head upright and facing forward.

Slowly shift back into *MaBu Zhuang*. As you raise your left fist to face your left cheek (with left elbow tucked in close to your body), drop your right fist under your left elbow. Straighten your left leg and turn your upper body toward the right as you twist your left forearm to bring your left fist close to your right cheek. Keep your head upright and facing forward.

Please practice this movement, alternating between the right and left sides, for at least 5–10 minutes.

Breath: Inhale as you contract toward the center and exhale as you expand away from the center.

Visualization: Imagine you are a huge bear backing into your cave as you practice this movement.

Figure 69: Kun—
right center

Figure 70: Kun—stretching right

Figure 71: Kun—left center

Figure 72: Kun—stretching left

Internal Alchemy Principle: This movement represents the trigram ☷ *Kun* (Earth). The *Kun* trigram is made of three broken Yin lines, and represents the earth, the vast open, straight, welcoming, center, and belly. In both martial arts and internal alchemy practice, the belly is the most important place of your body. This is where your power arises and where internal transformation occurs. As LaoZi states in his *DaoDeJing*: *ShengRenWeiFuBuWeiMu* 聖人為腹不為目[8]—The sage's [or enlightened being's] only focus is the belly and not the eyes. The guiding tenet of all internal cultivation is to bring your awareness back to your *DanTian*, not to focus on the external world by looking outside of yourself. He goes on to tell us: *XuQiXinShiQiFu* 虛其心實其腹[9]—Empty the heart to fill up your belly. When your Heart-Mind is emptied of the distractions of daily life, the Qi will naturally flow into your *DanTian*. This practice helps us to refine our *DanTian* Qi and bolsters our life source.

In the northern direction or bottom-most position of the *BaGua* diagrams, we can locate the trigrams *Kan*/Water and *Kun*/Earth. The combination of these trigrams makes the hexagram ䷇ *Bi* 比—Intimate. With time, you will find that this practice creates harmonious Qi in all areas of your life, allowing you to develop stronger and deeper connections with the different aspects of yourself as well as with your family and closest friends.

Martial Arts Principle: This movement helps to fortify your courage, which is especially beneficial when developing your close-up fighting skills. When your opponent starts to attack, this movement teaches you how to move in even closer in order to overthrow him. We commonly say this skill is *DaRenRuQingZui* 打人如親嘴—like beating others with what looks like a kiss. This martial arts principle is called *GuiDongFa* 歸洞瀘—The Method of Returning to the Cave.

---

8   Found in Chapter 12 of the *DaoDeJing*.
9   Found in Chapter 3 of the *DaoDeJing*.

Afterword
Master the One

For over ten years, my master, Zhao ShouRong 趙守榮, has been urging me to write this book and share Dai Family XinYi with the world at large. After many years of carefully considering how to best offer a clear picture of such an elegant and powerful internal alchemy–martial arts system, I have finally written this book to connect Daoist internal alchemy and the true spirit of traditional Chinese martial arts.

In this project, it felt very important that I focus on *WuDao* 武道, the way of martial arts, as opposed to *WuShu* 武術, the technique of martial arts. The Dao is unlimited and is the source of the *Shu*, whereas *Shu* is the expression of the Dao. From the perspective of Daoist numerology, Dao is One and *Shu* is innumerable. In martial arts, the Dao of a movement is the principle, which gives birth to the *Shu*—the numerous methods and applications of combat skills. If you are limited to knowing only one application of a movement without knowing the underlying principle, you will likely totally miss many other applications of the same movement. If the Dao is like the trunk of a tree, the *Shu* are the branches. To understand the One is the way to master the infinite.

I hope this book will bring you a new perspective of traditional Chinese martial arts, fill your daily cultivation with fresh Qi, and help you experience WuDao.

Purity Qi,

Master Zhongxian Wu   吳忠賢

Mid-Autumn, Year of Yin Water Snake   癸巳仲秋
Phoenix Nest, Sweden   於瑞典鳳棲巢